ARK FEVER

RoBeRT CoRNuKe

TYNDALE HOUSE PUBLISHERS, INC., WHEATON, ILLINOIS

Visit Tyndale's exciting Web site at www.tyndale.com

TYNDALE is a registered trademark of Tyndale House Publishers, Inc.

Tyndale's quill logo is a trademark of Tyndale House Publishers, Inc.

Ark Fever

Designed by Luke Daab

Edited by Dave Lindstedt and Linda Schlafer

Library of Congress Cataloging-in-Publication Data

Cornuke, Robert, date.
  Ark fever / Robert Cornuke.
    p. cm.
  ISBN-13: 978-1-4143-0296-6 (sc)
  ISBN-10: 1-4143-0296-7 (sc)
  1. Noah's ark. 2. Cornuke, Robert, date. —Travel—Turkey—Ararat, Mount. 3. Ararat, Mount (Turkey)—Description and travel. 4. Cornuke, Robert, 1951- —Travel—Iran. 5. Iran—Description and travel. I. Title.
BS658.C67 2005
222'.11093—dc22
                                       2005513140

Printed in the United States of America

11 10 09 08 07 06 05
7   6   5   4   3   2

To Edgar and Yvonne Miles.
I could never express in mere
words the appreciation I have for
your friendship and unflagging
support. This book is dedicated
to both of you.

CONTENTS

FOREWORD

Few people would deny that the actual discovery of Noah's ark would rock the archaeological world and cause many skeptics to take a renewed look at the truth and historical veracity of the Bible. Dr. Melville Bell Grosvenor, the late editor of *National Geographic,* once said, "If the ark of Noah is discovered, it will be the greatest archaeological find in human history, the greatest event since the resurrection of Christ, and it would alter all the currents of scientific thought."[1] With so much importance associated with an actual verified finding of Noah's ark, there is little wonder as to why ark devotees often succumb to a malady known as *ark fever.*

Ark fever strikes in various forms, and its symptoms range from an acute interest in finding the remains of Noah's ark to a full-blown, fever-pitched obsession. At its most severe, ark fever can cause otherwise sane people to see what they want to see—or expect to see—rather than what's really there. It's similar to *buck fever,* its close counterpart in deer season, which causes some hunters to mistake cows or other animals for deer. A cow looks very different from a deer, but the hunter sees only four legs and brown hair in his sights. In his eagerness to bag a buck, his mind convinces his eyes that the cow is a deer.

So it is with ark fever. Over the past two centuries, scores of climbers have scanned the rugged upper reaches of Mount Ararat with binoculars, espied a flat-edged stone slab jutting out of the snow, and exhaled in amazement, "It's the ark! I see it . . . don't you?" When ark fever strikes, your mind whispers, *It's there, it just has to be there.* I have personally seen this happen several times.

Afterward, the victim has an almost insatiable want or need to climb up the mountain and find the tantalizing apparition. Nothing short of actually standing on the suspected object or seeing it up close will convince these eyewitnesses that all they have discovered is just another unusual rock formation.

Today, with the advent of high-resolution satellite photographs, ark searchers do not even need to climb the mountain to find the ark. Over the past several years, countless people have placed magnifying glasses to their eyes and slowly scanned over satellite photographs of Mount Ararat in Turkey—and suddenly they see it: a shadowy, barge-like form that emerges from the grainy images of ice and shadows.

Unfortunately, none of the many expeditions to Mount Ararat turned up any verifiable evidence that the ark still exists. But the media have continued to print and broadcast the various sightings, and the search has continued.

With so many dead ends, disappointing expeditions, and false sightings over the past twenty years of my search for the ark, I lost interest along the way. My own ark fever dissolved into remission. But recent new discoveries have rekindled the fire of debate, and my temperature has started to rise again. Come with me now as we attempt to unlock a mystery as old as recorded history. But first a warning: What you are about to read may cause you to get a case of ark fever.

Robert Cornuke
Colorado Springs, Spring 2005

ACKNOWLEDGMENTS

The passage of time is cruel to anyone searching for hidden clues to our ancient past. With the passing of each day, each decade, and each century, the trail to truth erodes and clues fade. It often takes grit and a steeled determination to forge ahead (often against the advice of scholars and public opinion). With a journey into the ever darkening veil of history, it takes the help of very special people. First and foremost, I would like to deeply thank my beautiful wife and wonderful children.

The list of researchers, teammates, and other contributors who helped in these expeditions and literary efforts is too great to properly thank here. I would, however, like to specially thank the following people for all they have done: David and Francie Halbrook, Barbara and Pete Leininger, Mike and Susan Barnes, Les and Ann Stevens, Ray and Carol Ardizzone, Ron and Tisha Hicks, Daniel and Carol Ayres, Jim and Mary Irwin, Bob Stuplich, Brian Park, Dave Banks, Ed Holroyd, Gary Longfellow, Darrell Scott, John Tomlin, Ken Durham, Chuck Aaron, John Macintosh, Bill Crouse, Nahid Noorani, Ali Farrokhroo, Brad Houston, Paul and Nancy Cornuke, John and Regina Cornuke, Bill Dodder, Rex Geissler, Ron and

Debbie Acton, Dr. Roy Knuteson, Steve Crampton, Doug Scherling, Mike Morrison, Larry Williams, J. O. and Marlene Stewart, Ed Davis, Jim and Penny Caldwell, Don Shockey, Laura Lisle, Fatima, George Kralick, Dan Toth, Dan and Melly McGivern, Dick Bright, Kim Orr, Jon Arnold, Tom and Kim Bengard, Gore-Tex and their amazing products, Larry Bollinger, Dave Pacanowsky, and Alton Gansky.

A very special word of appreciation goes to Jon Farrar, Mary Keeley, Linda Schlafer, Dave Lindstedt, Erin Laning, and everyone at Tyndale House Publishers who had a part. Your contributions and direction made all this possible.

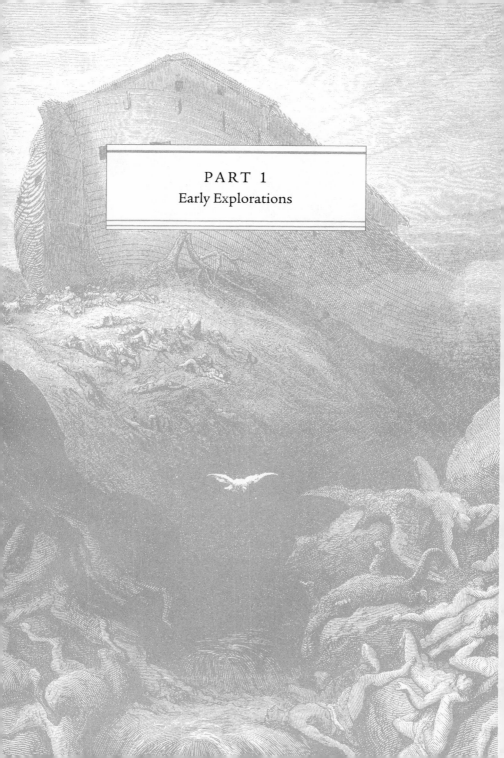

PART 1
Early Explorations

CHAPTER 1
HOW I CAUGHT ARK FEVER

Mount Ararat, Turkey, August 1982

Former Apollo astronaut James Irwin was above a treacherous northern chute high on Mount Ararat when he stopped, unable to descend further. His heart thumped against his rib cage as he gulped in the cold, thin mountain air.

The cumbersome metal crampons lashed to his boots had worked great up on the glacier, their steel fangs biting clean into the slick slab of ice. But now, as he was about to cross a boulder field on his way down to base camp, the crampons would be of no use. He sat down on a spine of rock jutting out from the snow and reached down to undo the leather straps that secured the crampons to his boots. He was irritated with himself because a few hours earlier he had failed in an attempt to reach the summit of

17,000-foot Mount Ararat. In frustration he had decided to leave the rest of the climb team and walk down to base camp alone.

He never arrived.

Mountaineering protocol dictates that climbers never go solo, and Irwin's uncharacteristic behavior had surprised the rest of the team. But Irwin was unaccustomed to defeat; after all, he had once planted an American flag in the gray dust of the moon.

A rock came loose from above and tumbled down the steep decline, clipping the base of Irwin's skull. He was sent cartwheeling like a rag doll down the craggy slope, eventually stopping on an ice-crusted rock field far below. Unconscious, his contorted body was a bloody mess. Four big gashes gouged his head, four teeth were knocked out, and his hands were cut so severely that they would swell to almost twice their normal size. His entire body was busted up, bludgeoned, sliced, and badly bruised.

When the rest of the team arrived at base camp and found that Irwin was missing, they searched for him into the night. Their headlamps groped the crags and sheer drop-offs for any sign of the famous astronaut in the inky blackness. But the terrain was too dangerous and steep, and they had to give up. They prayed all through the long, freezing night and hoped for the best, but everyone knew that other climbers had gone missing on these unforgiving slopes, never to be seen again.

When Irwin came to, writhing in pain and shivering from an icy wind, he somehow managed to get his backpack off and remove his sleeping bag. Ever so slowly, he shinnied inside the sleeping bag and rolled a few feet to a sheltered spot behind a big rock. Just then, a boulder dislodged from above and rumbled down the mountainside, colliding with Irwin's stone shield. The sound of the thunderous concussion was the last thing he remembered before lapsing into unconsciousness again.

The rescue team found him about eight o'clock the next morning. His sleeping bag was soaked in frozen blood, and the fabric had to be literally peeled away from his body. The Turkish commandos escorting the climbing group knew that if Irwin was to have any chance of survival, he needed to get off the big mountain soon.

While several of the climbers attended to Irwin's numerous injuries, one of the commandos hiked to a nearby village of nomadic Kurds living in tents. The soldier frantically requested that the Kurdish elder provide a donkey to carry the injured astronaut down to a hospital, but the elder refused to help. The Kurds hate the Turks and were not willing to cooperate.

Enraged and desperate, the Turkish soldier pressed a pistol to the Kurdish leader's forehead and threatened to kill everyone in the village and burn their tents if they would not comply.

The donkey was quickly made available, and Jim Irwin was soon brought down to a road where a car was flagged down to drive him to a medical facility. Somehow, he survived.

Colorado Springs, Winter 1985
When I first met Jim Irwin, I noticed a gray-white scar above his eyebrow, an indelible memento from his mountain accident three years earlier. We were in a restaurant having lunch with a small group of his family and friends. At the time, I was grappling with a strange midlife crisis. I had recently made a sudden, jarring exit

from law enforcement after a ten-year career. After moving my family from Southern California to Colorado, my snap decision to quit police work and go into real estate left me badly disoriented, wrestling with withdrawal from the excitement of my former job and yearning for something to fill the gap. But what could replace the sense of adventure and accomplishment I had enjoyed all those years as a cop?

I eased into the booming Colorado real estate market of the mid-1980s as a private developer. My brother Paul and I carved out a successful business in Colorado Springs. It got off to a fast start and occupied my days, but I still felt a hollow place in my chest just below where my badge had been.

I was presenting a talk one day to the Colorado Springs Board of Realtors when I met a man who said that he knew Jim Irwin, the famous *Apollo 15* astronaut. I had heard of Irwin, of course, and knew that he lived in Colorado Springs. I had also seen news reports of his expeditions to look for Noah's ark. When the man mentioned that he thought Irwin was planning another trip to Turkey to look for the ark, I asked him if he could arrange a meeting. Surprisingly, he agreed.

Jim and I hit it off immediately. He was a humble guy, lacking the self-importance that his astounding résumé might be expected to bring out. He put me at ease, conversing easily about a variety of topics, including his historic space flight and trip to the moon. At one point, he told me about a life-changing experience he'd had on the lunar surface that set the future course of his life's pursuit and inspired his belief in the truth of the Bible.

"David Scott and I were busy taking soil samples," he said, "collecting rocks, doing an endless list of tasks. It was a pretty tough pace, and we were sweating buckets from the glaring sun. I stood up for a moment to rest, turned around, and there was the earth, hanging like a droplet of water in the black vacuum of space. It looked misty, framed in bright greens, blues, and whites—like it was breathing."

He paused. "I felt like I was standing on the threshold of infinity and staring back at a little round ball of life that could only have been fashioned by the hand of an infinitely wise Creator. It wasn't a cosmic accident. I realized in that instant that there was a God and that there was a higher purpose for my life.

"When I got back to Earth, I felt it was time for some new goals. It's my calling now to give believers—and unbelievers—solid evidence of the Bible."

After Jim retired from NASA, he formed the High Flight Foundation, a nonprofit ministry based in Colorado Springs that channeled resources into searching for lost biblical sites and artifacts, including Noah's ark.

I admired his conviction, but I wasn't quite sure what to make of a famous astronaut investing his life in search of a legendary old boat. Nevertheless, the appeal of the adventure drew me in.

After lunch, Jim turned to me and said, "I hear you were a policeman—a SWAT team member—and that you've been shot at and had to shoot back. I also hear you were trained to handle hostile situations."

"Uh, yeah," I said. I didn't know why he'd be interested in my past.

"Someday I might need someone like you to go with me to the eastern frontier of Turkey. That country has been in ethnic turmoil, with Kurds fighting against Turks in a bloody civil war that has gone on for generations. I would want a guy like you along, just in case."

Several weeks later, Jim Irwin called me and asked if I'd be interested in helping him raise the funds needed for another exploratory trip to Turkey.

"Sure," I said. "I'd love to be a part of something like that." I had no idea *how,* but I was getting my first taste of ark fever.

I recruited my brother to help me raise some money for the High Flight Foundation. We decided to build a house and donate the profits. Paul and I put up the project money and used our contacts to get discounts on labor and materials. The house, which we called "The Noah's Ark House," sold quickly, and we turned a tidy profit. The day after the closing, I handed Jim Irwin a $15,000 check. The next day, he invited me to join the expedition to climb the massive Mount Ararat in Turkey. I jumped at the opportunity.

A climb of that magnitude requires some serious training, so even though spending long hours punishing my body has never been my idea of fun, I jogged mile after mile down lonely mountain roads and spent weekends on training climbs up icy mountain peaks in the Colorado Rockies.

Because I didn't know the first thing about mountain climbing, I enlisted the help of two experienced climbers, a couple of free-spirited guys from a neighboring town. Together, we climbed Pike's Peak in a snowstorm, and a few weeks later we trudged through waist-deep snow to the top of Mount Quandary.

On my last training climb, the three of us tackled some steep cliffs above Leadville, Colorado. One of the climbers, a guy named Steve, tied off on a boulder as he prepared to rappel down a forty-foot rock face. It had rained the night before, and when Steve was just over the edge of the cliff, the egg-shaped rock he had used for his anchor hold rotated in its muddy base, releasing the rope. Steve fell. I was right below him, standing next to the other climber, but all we could do was watch helplessly as Steve plummeted onto a rocky ledge. I heard the sickening sound of his leg snapping as he flipped backward and careened down a patch of dirty summer snow, coming to a hard stop on some rocks.

Steve lay there, his foot and lower ankle bent sideways. The other climber began to panic when he stared down at Steve's mangled leg. The sight sickened him, and he could hardly draw a breath. I seized him by the collar and looked him in the face. "Don't lose it now," I ordered.

I stabilized and splinted Steve's leg as best I could and asked him whether he could handle the pain if we carried him out. He nodded, but I could see in his twisted expression that he was suffering unimaginably. I didn't want to leave him with the other climber who by now was walking around in circles, hyperventilating.

It had taken us a couple of hours of climbing to get to where we were, and I was disoriented because I had not been paying attention to landmarks along the way. I learned a big lesson in what not to do on a mountain. I had assumed that Steve would guide us out because he knew the area well, but he was of little help now.

The sun was setting behind the snowcapped peaks, and I couldn't tell which of my companions was worse off. With darkness fast descending, we decided to get Steve down as best we could.

Six hours later, exhausted beyond description, we finally reached the car, and Steve was soon in emergency care at a local hospital.

After hearing about Jim Irwin's fall—and now witnessing Steve's—I was fast learning that mountains are unforgiving and dangerous. I knew that Mount Ararat would test me to my limits.

CHAPTER 2
THE EYEWITNESS

Farmington, New Mexico, June 1986

In one of several conversations I had with Jim Irwin in the months leading up to the Turkish expedition, he suggested that I attend a convention of Noah's ark researchers, dubbed the "Arkathon," in Farmington, New Mexico. Because I would be making my maiden journey to Mount Ararat, Jim figured I could use some indoctrination in contemporary ark lore.

I had my doubts, imagining a gathering of wild-eyed, Bible-thumping zealots. But I had nothing to fear. Most of the participants were scholarly and mild-mannered educators, businessmen, tradesmen, or pastors who all shared a singular interest in finding Noah's ark. Some had spent years researching the topic and clearly looked forward to dissecting all the theories, tracking the scholarly record, and submitting their own hypotheses. Many had climbed huge mountains in the Middle East, bringing back mysterious reports. Others had built detailed scale models or sketched thoughtful portraits of eyewitness "sightings." The mood throughout the conference seemed focused and cooperative, which I attributed to its evangelical bent.

Toward the end of the convention, Don Shockey, one of the organizers of the event, introduced a dignified, older gentleman, who, he said, had "a unique testimony."

Ed Davis shuffled slowly down the aisle to the podium. His posture bent by age, he cut an eccentric figure in his cowboy boots, gray cowboy hat, bolo tie, and gaudy, turquoise-encrusted belt buckle. But once he opened his mouth and started talking, he transformed the conference. In a raspy, homespun, matter-of-fact voice, he made a convincing case that he had seen an enormous old boat high on a mountain somewhere in the Middle East. Standing there unruffled, and with a trace of dry humor, he recounted an incredible journey he had taken fifty years earlier as a U.S. Army sergeant stationed in Iran.

I sat transfixed as he described the arduous climb up the mountain to see the ark. The way he narrated the journey—describing the native garb and religious customs of his Iranian guides, recalling the texture of the cave walls, the smell of sulfur in the village, the hue and contour of the terrain, even the way the clouds hung and the sun angled in the sky the afternoon he spied the ark—all conveyed the sort of esoteric detail that one wouldn't think to include if he hadn't actually visited the place. No one at the conference knew what to think. Most of us had never heard anyone say he had actually "seen" the ark. By the time Ed Davis finished, the electricity in the air was palpable.

At the time, I thought the old man was delusional or crazed from a rabid case of ark fever. I'd heard some tall tales as a cop, and this one was way over the top. But I had also never heard such a grandiose story told with such sincerity and unwavering surety. Ed Davis had little proof of what he saw way back in 1943—other than the warranty of his long and honest life—but among ark researchers, his amazing story is by far the most famous of all sightings.

ED DAVIS'S STORY

During World War II, Sergeant Ed Davis and his unit, the 363rd Army Corps of Engineers, worked out of Hamadan, Iran. The corps' mission in Iran was to help the British and Soviet armies build a supply corridor from the Persian Gulf to Russia. Davis soon befriended a young Iranian truck driver named Badi, who was assigned to taxi military supplies and personnel across the countryside.

One afternoon, as they loaded trucks at a rock quarry near Hamadan, Davis asked Badi where he lived.

Badi pointed toward a great mountain range off in the distance. "That's where I grew up," Badi said. "The mountain holds a sacred secret. Beneath a glacier near the peak is the ark of Noah."

Davis raised an eyebrow. "Noah's ark?"

Badi was adamant. "My family has been to the ark. My grandfather has taken me up to see it."

It was an intriguing claim, and Davis expressed interest in seeing the ark some day, but he gave the matter no more thought until, weeks later, an elderly Iranian showed up at the base looking for Badi. The visitor was Abas, Badi's father, who had come down from the mountains with news for his son, whom he eventually found in

Davis's company. Over the course of several days, Abas confirmed his son's comments about the ark and described in detail the artifacts he had found scattered around the ancient relic, some of which he claimed to have in his possession at home.

These discussions continued to pique Davis's imagination, but he remained skeptical until the day when Abas arrived in camp again.

"The ice on the big mountain has melted considerably," Abas said. "Part of the ark is showing." After a long pause, he added, "If you like, I can take you there."

It seemed to Davis a dubious enterprise at best. He wasn't even certain that he believed in the story of Noah's ark and the great Flood. But he liked traveling to new places, and an adventure in Iran's hinterlands appealed to him. He secured a short leave of absence to accompany his friend to the sacred mountain. A few days later, they got supplies—three barrels of gas, a case of motor oil, and some coffee—and set out from Hamadan in an army-issued truck. They drove all day and much of the night without the benefit of a map. Davis noted a number of Russian encampments on the route north and paid casual notice to a town Badi pointed out called "Cazbeen."

They arrived at Abas's village early in the evening. The mud and rock buildings reminded Davis of the adobe pueblos he knew back home in Albuquerque. Abas's relatives welcomed Davis as a member of the family, and after a dinner of stew, the patriarch told Davis, "I have some items out back that might interest you. Please come and take a look."

Davis felt his pulse quicken as Abas led him to a nearby shed and opened the door. Abas pulled an unwieldy object from the shadows. As Davis's eyes adjusted to the dark, he realized that he was looking at a door about three feet tall. On closer inspection, Davis recognized it as an incredibly old cage door. Its vertical bars were woven of twisted branches, now hard as a rock.

Abas then showed Davis an array of ancient-looking oil lamps, old clay vats, bowls, jars, and crude tools, with a stash of what appeared to be prehistoric farm implements. Abas explained that villagers had collected these and other artifacts in the high canyon where the ark lay.

It surprised Davis to learn that no other Westerner had ever seen these articles; it startled him even more to hear that he must keep this all to himself.

"The ark and its contents have always been considered sacred by our people," Abas explained. "Outsiders would only steal or profane them. For that reason, they have been kept hidden from the outside world."

The statement confused Davis. Why should he be trusted with such a secret? When they retired for the night, Davis slept restlessly. He wondered what other surprises the countryside held.

In the middle of the night, Davis woke to loud shouts and banging outside his door. "Wake up! Wake up! We go! We go!"

He rose, tired and stiff, to see Abas, Badi, and seven of Badi's brothers loading supplies into the truck. Within minutes, the band of adventurers had loaded up and driven off to travel through the predawn night.

In the first light of morning, they arrived at a primitive-looking village in the shadow of the great mountains Badi had described. Davis noticed a peculiar vineyard around the village. It had an ancient, arthritic appearance, with vines and trunks so thick and tangled that a grown man would have trouble reaching his arms around them.

They look as old as time itself, Davis thought.

After a breakfast of stew, Davis, Badi, and his family mounted packhorses and began the long, grueling trek up the mountain.

DAVIS'S HIGH ADVENTURE

A series of hidden caves provided shelter and support along the arduous route up the peak. By late afternoon they reached the first cave, cloistered in a maze of low ravines deep in the foothills. After a quick meal, they mounted again and rode higher up a narrow mountain trail called the "Back Door" that was frequented by bandits and black marketers. Rounding a steep, blind bend, Davis saw a pair of decomposing human legs, frozen and half-buried in a snowbank. The brothers barely acknowledged it.

"He shouldn't have been up here," they remarked. Davis suddenly felt vulnerable and out of his element.

The route turned treacherous. Endless hairpin switchbacks up an increasingly sharp grade made for slippery footing. The awkward gait of the spindly Iranian horses set Davis's teeth on edge as they skirted the razor edges of sheer cliffs. A cold, numbing rain never stopped, but still they climbed, traversing one hair-raising ridge after another. Late in the day, the trail ended at a huge rock slide.

Are we there? Davis wondered. His heart sank as one of Badi's brothers led the horses away, confirming that the next part of the journey would be on foot. They roped themselves together and strained higher into the wet, foggy haze. Just before nightfall, they arrived at a second, larger cave and spent the night resting.

The next morning, the party waited for a dense mantle of clouds and rain to dissipate before setting off. An overwhelming stench of sulfur hung in the air. Time passed slowly for Davis on these heights, and he felt relieved when the clouds parted and they could continue their journey.

The terrain turned more severe, and again they roped themselves together to scale an increasingly chaotic tangle of narrow ledges, steep ridges, and high cliffs. At one point, the brothers clapped their hands over their mouths and ordered Davis to be still.

"Russian sentries stationed below," Abas whispered, pointing. "They would not be pleased by our presence."

From then on, no one said a word. The brothers communicated by a series of hand gestures, clipped snorts, and whistles. They eventually reached a third cave, where another steaming pot of goulash awaited. Davis wondered who prepared these meals and felt indebted to the phantom chef. Settling in for the night, Davis believed that they might have climbed higher but for the Soviet soldiers on the mountain.

On the third day, climbing became harder and more perilous. The group made most of its final dizzying turns tethered together by lengthy ropes, pulling one another up and over the sharp ledges. Passing into another dense canopy of cloud, the group reached a precariously perched cave hidden from the persistent rain that often turned to sleet. Davis wanted nothing more than to collapse, but he couldn't help gazing at the cave walls, adorned with strange writings and etchings of oddly pigmented animals. Davis marveled at their ancient appearance and wondered what this place was as he drifted into sleep.

The next morning, the skies were gray and again laden with rain. Storms and lightning kept the group cave-bound until early afternoon, when a short break finally appeared in the clouds. They mustered their gear and made a frantic scramble up and over the last perilous pitch, a jagged moraine called Doomsday Point. The bulbous outcropping dropped off on one side into a mile-deep chasm. Abas said that it had taken the life of many a weary climber.

"IT'S ENORMOUS!"

Edging heel-to-toe past the terrible drop-off, Davis found himself balanced on a ledge that overlooked a deep, horseshoe-shaped gorge, its belly socked in by a dense cloud bank. They could see almost nothing, which meant more waiting and wondering for Davis as to what lay below. Abas and his clan whiled away the hours by chattering aimlessly and flapping their arms to stay warm. Davis stood to the side, lost in his thoughts.

Just before dusk, as the group prepared to abandon the day's mission, a flare of sunlight broke through the clouds, and Davis caught his first glimpse of the shadowy canyon. Badi and his brothers quietly began to pray, whispering petitions to Allah. Davis stood to the side, unsure what to do, when Abas walked him over to the ledge and pointed down.

"There it is," he told Davis. "Noah's ark."

For several moments, they looked into the gorge.

"Do you see it?" Abas asked.

It took Davis's eyes a minute to adjust as he stared hard into the yawning chasm. He saw only heavy, formless shadows. Rocks, ice, and the mountainside melded as one in the darkness.

Davis turned in frustration to Abas. "No. Nothing but shadows."

"Look again."

After more tense moments of staring into the darkness, the murky shadow at last yielded form and depth. An angular object, strangely out of place among ice-polished boulders, emerged like a leviathan floating up from the abyss. Suddenly he saw a huge rectangular structure lying on its side, like a battleship stuck on a sandbar.

"I see it," said Davis. "It's . . . it's enormous!"

After another few seconds, as his eyes adjusted to the shadowy surroundings, he could see the ark's full form and detail. Its bow, partially covered by a talus of snow and ice, appeared blunt and battered but suggested a rugged, majestic symmetry. There could be no doubt about it—this had to be a wooden ship, somehow marooned high on this ice-capped mountain.

Davis blinked, then realized that he was looking *into* the craft, its dark, yawning maw stretching one hundred feet into the cleft of ice. Twisted, gnarled timbers splintered up and out, framing the hole where the hull had split apart.

"Look down there," Abas instructed, pointing at another object further down the gorge. About half a mile from the main section, another massive structure had settled in among the boulders, its timbers ripped and protruding at one end, exactly like the section still embedded in the ice. It was clear that the pieces had once been connected.

Further down the gorge lay more pieces of the ship, some sections wedged between rocks, some bathed in glacial snowmelt. The ice had receded just enough to expose what had lain entombed for ages.

"For ten, twenty years at a time," Abas said, "the ark lies invisible under the ice. Then suddenly it appears."

Davis rubbed his eyes, gazing deeper still into the cross-section of the main hull. He wondered at the craft's intricate interior design, with its three distinct floors, some parts of which seemed to have collapsed. On the upper deck sat a raised roof, an elongated ridge running the better part of the ship's length.

Davis craned his neck over the ledge, willing himself closer to the legendary artifact. His hands shook, partly from the cold, but more from the surge of adrenaline pulsing through his limbs.

A freezing rain began to fall again, soaking his parka and stinging his nose. Davis remained heedless to all but the overpowering thought of climbing down into the canyon. He desperately wanted to touch the ark, as if physical contact would confirm its reality.

A HAUNTING MEMORY

"Come, my friend," Abas whispered. "We must leave. We will return tomorrow."

Davis didn't want to go. He could have stared at the ark forever. It had taken everything he had to make it this far; how could he just leave? Reason told him that what lay below could not exist—it must be a hallucination. An enormous ship resting near the summit of a towering peak? Davis couldn't bring himself to believe that it really was Noah's ark, yet there it sat, clear as day. What else could it be?

It was almost within reach.

Davis tried to ignore the rain, sleet, and cold. At any minute, he knew, the rain would become snow, turning the steep slope into an ice rink. He had been standing almost motionless for over an hour. He stared at the big boat, taking in its every detail and memorizing the scene. Abas beckoned again; the weather refused to wait and they had to leave.

Taking Davis by the arm, Abas coaxed him away from the ledge. Before joining his friends on their careful descent, Davis made Abas promise they would come back.

"Tomorrow, we must return."

"We will come back first thing in the morning," Abas assured him. "You can inspect it for yourself firsthand."

They descended the embankment to a cave on the peak's wind-swept face. The exhausting, precarious hike had left them chilled to the bone. A warm fire crackled inside, and a cast-iron stew pot simmered over smoking coals. They devoured the food and crawled into their bedrolls, but Davis couldn't sleep. His stomach churned, and haunting thoughts that he might never see the ark again kept him awake.

The next day, the weather remained cold and rainy, and the fog-filled gorge allowed them only brief, distant glimpses of the ark. Still, Davis was insistent that he wanted to touch the ark. When sleeting rain mixed with snow covered the rock face with a glaze of ice wisdom decreed a rapid descent.

With hardly a nod to the building storm, they bundled up and bound themselves to a length of rope, marching methodically back up to the canyon through a swelling blizzard. The ark was once again entombed beneath an icy shroud. The mountain had reclaimed its prize, and Noah's boat had resumed its hibernation among the rocky clefts. Davis felt distraught; he knew he had seen the last of the ark.

WHO WOULD BELIEVE IT?

Traveling through heavy snow and relentless rain, the party eventually arrived, bruised and battered, at Abas's village. Davis said his good-byes and returned to his unit via Tehran. His attempts to describe his exploits provoked jeering skepticism from his army buddies. Not even his closest friends took him seriously. Some shrugged politely and turned away; others mocked him or laughed in his face.

"Show us pictures," they demanded. "Tell us more about your ghosts and phantom boats."

Humiliated, the shy sergeant vowed never again to speak with strangers about what he had seen. He solemnly wrote the following inscription in his Bible, including the date of his discovery:

> Went to Ararat with Abas. We saw a big ship on a ledge in two pieces. I stayed with him at the big house. It rained and snowed for ten days. I stopped in Tehran and got some supplies and got warm and rested up. Lt. Burt was glad I got back. He was scared for me. He was afraid I would get killed, I think. I am glad I went. I think it is the ark. Abas has lots of things from there. My legs are almost healed from the horseback ride.
>
> Ed Davis

Soon after Davis returned from the mountain, the army transferred him to other parts of the Middle East. After a second tour of duty, serving under General Patton in France, during which he received four battle stars, a bronze star, and a silver star for his war efforts, he was shipped home to Albuquerque. He never returned to

Iran, and he didn't discuss his adventure with anyone else for the remainder of the war.

For the next forty years, he lived in peaceful obscurity, working at the Bandelier National Monument near Los Alamos and as an inspector for twenty years in Sandia Base, New Mexico. After retirement Davis raised prized Nubian goats. Seldom did he mention his journey up the mountain. But Ed Davis could never shake the memory of the ark. It haunted his dreams each night for the rest of his life.[1]

CHAPTER 3

BUSTED IN ERZURUM

Erzurum, Turkey, August 1986

Shortly after attending the Arkathon, I went to Turkey with Jim Irwin and a small group of explorers to look for Noah's ark on Mount Ararat. We landed in Ankara and headed for Erzurum, the closest major city to the mountain, which sits on the eastern Turkish frontier.

In preparation for our climb, pilot Dick Bright and two Dutch photographers flew a rented Cessna 206 around Mount Ararat on a scouting mission. They made several passes around the mountain, capturing points of interest on film. The rest of us waited anxiously at the airport for their return.

When Bright was on his approach to the Erzurum airport, the Turkish secret police radioed him and told him he couldn't land because the airport was "closed for the night."

"That's absurd," Bright erupted over the radio. "Do they expect us to stay in the air all night?"

Eventually, he brought the plane down with little fuel left and was stunned when the authorities denied ever giving him permission to take off in the first place. To top it off, the Turks accused him of violating Russian and Iranian airspace, an infraction nearly impossible to monitor or prove. The nonsensical allegations earned us a rude escort back to our hotel, where we were placed under house arrest.

Hounded by worry, I couldn't get the prison scenes from *Midnight Express* out of my mind. I kept watching Jim Irwin, who appeared calm, almost indifferent about this latest turn of events. With more than fifty machine-gun-wielding policemen waiting in the street below, he simply said, "Tell the truth."

We discussed the importance of retrieving the film the police had taken from us because we knew they could doctor it and use it as evidence against us. Besides, without the photos from the flight around Mount Ararat, our trip would be a total loss. The film was in our backpacks in an adjacent room, along with all our equipment. One of us would have to get into the room unnoticed, retrieve the film, and get out without the guards catching him. Expedition climber Bob Stuplich volunteered, and the chore of distraction fell to fellow teammate Bill Dodder and me. The three of us quickly devised a plan for diverting the attention of the young guard outside our room.

Splashing water on my face to simulate sweat, I grabbed a handful of blueberry granola and stuffed it in my mouth. Then we stepped into the hall and walked slowly toward the guard. Before he could react, Stuplich started waving frantically, pointing at me and yelling, "We need help. . . . Please, help us." On cue, I doubled over and pretended to throw up, spewing half-chewed blueberry granola all over the corridor. Then I fell to the floor, writhing and moaning as if my appendix had burst.

While the guard rushed to my aid, eyes bulging with fright, Stuplich slid into the unlocked room, rifled through the bags, and found the film. He stuffed several rolls in his coat pocket, replaced them with unused canisters, and calmly reappeared, quiet as a cat. The whole transaction took only seconds. I stood up, shook myself off, and bowed to the confused guard. We scurried back to our room, leaving the guard in the hall rubbing his head, unsure of what he had just seen.

Most of our film was eventually returned to us anyway, and the whole arrest fiasco was dismissed somehow, but for a novice like me, outwitting Turkey's elite secret police was exciting stuff. It made me think that I could do this explorer gig. Something about the intrigue, the risk, and the uncertainty of the hunt appeased my wanderlust. Although we didn't get to climb Mount Ararat, I left Turkey with a desire to come back and try again to find the ark. I had the fever.

TOO BIG FOR THE GAME

After the arrest, Jim Irwin never again took an ark exploration trip to Turkey. His presence had turned what should have been a low-key, under-the-radar expedition into a media circus with reporters and photographers hovering like vultures to get close to the "great American astronaut." Recent trips had been maddening drills in waiting, wondering, begging, and bargaining just to obtain a climbing permit. With Jim present, it had become almost impossible.

It was an interesting paradox. The Turkish public at first hailed Jim as a hero, but the government officials became suspicious and feared that the famous astronaut might perish on their mountain. Jim's prominence had opened Turkey's closed doors to research expeditions in 1982, but subsequent to that his presence made it extremely difficult to gain government approval to climb Mount Ararat, a politically sensitive mountain on the borders of Iran and Armenia.

Jim was at peace with his decision not to venture into Turkey again. He'd given it his best shot, used his influence with integrity, and had become an unflagging ambassador of goodwill between the United States and Turkey. He'd gone the extra mile in search of the ark, almost killing himself in that spectacular fall.

CHAPTER 4

THE POLYGRAPH

Turkey, August 1987

It seemed impossible, but the year after our aborted trip to Mount Ararat, we were back in Turkey for another attempt at the mountain. This time, we had actually received permission to use a helicopter. To the best of my knowledge, no one had ever flown a helicopter expedition around the famous peak.

In a helicopter, you can see more terrain in a minute than you can in a month on foot. I remember thinking that this was the year we would find the old boat, and I would be there to see it, along with Bob Stuplich, who was also back for another try.

The only problem this time was the weather. Brooding, swollen clouds cloaked the mountain for days, and the snow piled high on Ararat's perpetual glaciers. We took off in the rented Bell Jet

Ranger and flew to within a few miles of the mountain, but all we really accomplished was to get above the clouds and snap a few shots of the white crown of snow blanketing Ararat's looming peak. After a short foray, our Turkish pilot, fearing worsening weather, circled around and landed back at the makeshift helipad at the base of the mountain. After waiting another day for the weather to improve, we canceled the expedition for the year.

We returned to the United States, disappointed by the results of our mission but encouraged that we had been given permission to fly around the mountain. Shortly thereafter, Jim Irwin introduced us to a successful commodities broker named Larry Williams, who he said might be willing to bankroll the next year's attempt at another helicopter flight. Larry is a brilliant businessman with a taste for adventure, and he and I would ultimately team up on a number of expeditions, including a journey to Saudi Arabia to search for the real Mount Sinai.

After hearing our plans, Larry agreed to fund the whole trip for 1988. Even though he would never admit it, I think Larry had gotten ark fever. His first suggestion was that we see if we could get Ed Davis to take a lie detector test.

"Let's find out if old Ed is telling the truth when he said he saw the ark way back in 1943," Larry said. When Ed agreed to take the test, I made arrangements to fly to New Mexico.

THE TEST
My plane landed in Albuquerque the morning of May 1, 1988. Ed Davis and Don Shockey met me at the airport, and we drove straight to the downtown offices of P.G.P. Polygraph.

Before the examination began, I took a few minutes with the examiner, P. G. Pierangel. He was crusty, rough, and ill-humored, but also a well-regarded authority on the standard Backster Tri-Zone Comparison Specific Examination. I knew that the test was only as good as the guy giving it, so I was reassured to find that Pierangel knew his stuff. With a cocky smirk, he assured me, "I've been doing this a long time. If he's lying, I'll break him."

Ed Davis seemed unusually stiff and uncomfortable. Since his performance at the Arkathon, his quiet life had changed. An aggressive new breed of ark searchers, as well as a flock of cynical reporters, had called him repeatedly at home, wanting to hear his story. Strangers showed up at his farm unannounced, asking him to affirm their wacky theories on everything from the great Flood to the Second Coming. Others, like me, wanted to strap him to a lie detector.

I felt guilty. Davis didn't need the attention or aggravation that a bad test score might arouse. He had lived a good life, and he had no use for meddlers who would question his motives and invade his privacy. Still, after almost half a century, the memory of the ark stuck with Davis like an old war injury. For forty-five years, it had haunted his dreams and invaded his private thoughts. Watching him remove his coat that day and carefully place his gray felt cowboy hat aside, I sensed that he had wrestled long with the idea of "coming out." He seemed resigned to his peculiar role in history, if not at ease with it. "If these youngsters really want to know about the ark," his tired eyes seemed to say, "I guess I'll oblige them."

We had worked up a comprehensive set of questions, and I went over the sequence with the examiner. After brief introductions, Davis and Pierangel sat down in the examination room—a stark, spartan office with the bare white walls typical of any police interrogation room in America. The preliminary interview began.

Davis dredged the recesses of his memory to recount the story, shifting his head this way and that as he spoke, turning the scene over in his mind, moving his legs and torso and consciously reenacting the whole episode. In his mind's eye, he saw and felt the mountain as it was on that day—the exact position of the ark, the falling snow, the rocks and sky—from his precarious perch on a ledge. It was an eerie thing to watch. He filled his descriptions with impeccable detail, and as he continued, Davis seemed to gain confidence, drawing energy and taking delight in recalling his story. Forty-five years after the fact, his audience still hung on every word.

Once the questioning began, Davis never wavered or waffled, though Pierangel grilled him repeatedly. Pierangel, a no-nonsense guy, was interested only in getting to the truth. His face betrayed the cynicism of his years of listening to lying thugs and conniving con artists. He came at Davis with a surly, accusing tone.

"Are you lying when you state that you were taken to Mount Ararat by Abas and his seven sons?

"Are you lying when you state that you climbed Mount Ararat on horseback and on foot?

"Are you lying when you state that you saw a large wooden structure high on Mount Ararat?"

Davis never stumbled. The polygraph needle never spiked. His answers indicated that he told the truth when he said that he had seen Noah's ark. Pierangel looked shocked and readministered the test to see if he might get different results.

After an hour, the examiner was visibly tired, but he kept repeating the mantra, "Let's run through this one more time." His expression changed from gritty determination to mild frustration to utter bewilderment. When the test finally ended, he slipped from the room, wiping sweat from his forehead and mumbling under his breath.

"I don't know if this guy saw Noah's ark or not," Pierangel said, "but I tell you what I do know—this old man *believes* he saw it. He definitely believes he saw a huge boat on top of a mountain. That much is fact."

Pierangel hustled out of the lobby, leaving Davis in the interview room. I waited a few minutes for the old man to collect himself, then I went in and sat down.

"Mr. Davis," I said, "could I have a few minutes alone with you?"

He nodded, and I closed the door. His face showed a man well into his twilight, but his eyes still gleamed like a child's, full of wonder. The test had worn him out, but he seemed relaxed, exhilarated, and ready for more. Sharing his story had been a much-needed emotional release.

"I hope they know now that I was telling the truth," he said, searching my eyes for a clue as to the results. "I hope I proved I'm not a senile old man."

"You passed with flying colors," I told him. He grinned with pride. "I need to ask you something, though—man to man," I said.

He eyed me for a moment, then said, "Go on, young man."

I reminded him that I would be going overseas soon to search for the ark. "I'm putting my family at risk," I said, watching the glint of his eye, "so with all due respect, sir, and in complete confidence, I need to know if you are even a little bit uncertain about what you saw. If so, then please tell me. It'll be between us. I won't repeat it or think less of you. If you're trying to save face, that's fine. But I have a wife and kids. I'm about to put my rear end on the line, and I need to know the truth."

It was an old police tactic, giving him an out—sort of like telling a shoplifter, "I'll just turn my head if you put the candy bar back." But Davis didn't want an out; his gaze remained unwavering.

He looked me squarely in the eye, smiled broadly, and in his typical unassuming fashion said, "You won't believe how big it is when you see it!"

A shiver trickled down my neck like ice water. I knew that Ed Davis had seen what he had seen, whatever it was, and I could take it or leave it. We shook hands. I thanked him for his patience and bid him a warm farewell. Watching him shuffle from the room, I felt a twinge of remorse. I wished I had gotten to know him better, on a different level.

As the door closed behind him, the reality hit me. This old man said that he had seen the ark, and the polygraph said he had told the truth—a stunning result. No one, to my knowledge, had ever passed a lie detector test while saying that they had actually seen Noah's ark. I was unprepared for it, and it knocked me off balance.

I walked to a phone and called Larry Williams. When he answered, I didn't even say hello.

"Larry, I don't know if Davis saw the boat or not, but he definitely *thinks* he saw it. He passed the lie detector test."

1988 HELICOPTER TOUR

After Ed Davis passed the lie detector test, Larry Williams was ready to spend whatever it took to get another helicopter in the air over Mount Ararat. It took months to get permits from the tangled Turkish bureaucracy, but eventually we got them. We then had to figure out a way to get a big helicopter and extra fuel across Turkey, which proved difficult.

In Erzurum, my brother Paul and I bought ten barrels of jet fuel at the local airport, rented a minivan, and made final preparations for a five-hour push across Turkey's eastern outback. Since we could find no metal drums for sale in town, we had to buy light-weight thirty-gallon drums with flimsy push-and-seal lids. These rubberized vats let fuel splash from their ill-fitting tops—a disaster in the making. It posed a serious problem for the long, bumpy ride ahead of us, but we had to make do.

The day before the flight over Ararat, we awoke at 4:00 AM and loaded the plastic drums into the bed of the van. The van came with a scrawny, toothless driver named Yavuz, who was dressed in a moth-eaten T-shirt and rubber sandals. We carefully informed Yavuz of the unstable and highly flammable nature of our cargo, then held our breath as he put the van in gear and steered out of town, accelerating slowly and methodically, and trying valiantly if unsuccessfully to maneuver around endless rocks and potholes. Each bump sent toxic whitecaps of jet fuel splashing across the floor of the van.

Within five miles of Erzurum, the fumes overcame Paul and me. The thick, caustic air sent vapor trails rippling out the windows. We had become a mobile Molotov cocktail looking for a target—a fact that escaped our driver. Less than twenty miles into the plain, Yavuz popped a cigarette into his mouth and started to strike a match. Paul and I lunged forward, screaming, "No-o-o-o-o!"

I grabbed Yavuz's hand before he sent us up in an orange and red mushroom cloud. "Fumes! *FUMES!*" I yelled, pinching my nose and waving a hand to make him understand. With a vacant grin, Yavuz nodded and kept driving, thereafter resisting the urge to smoke.

We located the helicopter, resting in a field at the base of Ararat, as planned. Chuck Aaron, our American pilot, emerged from behind the chopper with a broad grin when I stepped out to greet him. He was glad the needed fuel had arrived.

"Ready to go find the ark?" he asked with his trademark smirk. I've seldom met anyone as arrogant and cocksure as Aaron. In the mid-1980s, everyone wanted this master pilot to fly their missions, and he had made more flights around Mount Ararat than any other American civilian pilot. Years later, Aaron set a chopper down at 16,000 feet on Ararat's windswept western plateau, an act of insane daring that set a world record for high-altitude landing. His reputation for skill and bravado put me at ease; I knew that in a pinch, he could make a chopper do the tango. Sure, Chuck Aaron was the first to claim that he was the best; but since I knew he could back it up, I was glad to let him wing us above Ararat's savage heights.

Using a small, hand-cranked pump, we spent the next hour filling the chopper's thirsty tanks from our plastic drums. Then Aaron lit up the Jet Ranger's engines and rechecked his gauges, while Larry Williams and I removed the doors and windows for maximum visibility and strapped ourselves in. I wore several layers of warm clothes, including three layers of pants. With the doors removed from the helicopter, the temperature would be well below zero at 16,000 feet.

Larry and I checked our seat belts one last time as the rotor blades began to spin, spooling up as they bit into the cool morning air and sending a hurricane blast through the open doors. I gave a thumbs-up signal to Paul, who was staying behind with the van in case the police showed up with questions about our activities. As

Chuck Aaron manipulated the controls, the whirring, 3,000-pound chopper lifted straight up and hovered about four feet off the ground.

His voice crackled over the headset, "You guys ready?"

We immediately answered, "Okay."

The craft tilted forward, taking off toward the 17,000-foot snowcapped mountain that filled the entire Plexiglas windshield. We had lifted off at 9:00 AM in a breathtaking blast of cold air.

As expected, the pristine weather gave us perfect visibility. Rising to 14,000 feet, we flew directly to Ararat's west glacier, where Italian explorer Angelo Palego claimed to have discovered Noah's ark.

Experts think that the glacier bed sits over a collapsed volcano cone. Some speculate that the ark may have come to rest here. Aaron ascended to 15,000 feet and let us look directly into the ice cap, which in places was more than 200 feet thick. During years of heavy melt-back like this one, the ice forms small pockets of water in whose glass-clear waters some have seen a shadowy, ark-like structure. Rolling deftly with the currents, Aaron feathered us down to within one hundred feet of the surface, giving us a straight-on view. We saw nothing—no shadow beneath the ice, no fuzzy image in the melting glacial waters. For the first time that day, I felt a tug of disappointment.

Aaron next took us up to the Cehennem Dere ice rim, swooping down and across the northeast ice cap known as the Abich II Glacier. Propped between Ararat's two peaks, Abich II forms a broad saddle that yields occasional sightings of a large, boxlike structure tucked beneath the ice and snow. Some think that the ark lies here, but once again, from our airborne perspective, we saw nothing.

I became concerned, then irritated. None of the promising land-marks yielded anything. Eyewitnesses swore that they had made compelling sightings here. Had they lied? Were they experiencing optical illusions? There couldn't have been clearer visibility, but as we skimmed the windswept peaks, the dry, brown mountain lacked anything remotely resembling a boat or pieces of wood. Still, I kept hoping.

One prominent feature still awaited our inspection: the big can-yon nestled deep within the Ahora Gorge. Aaron slanted the heli-copter sideways and dove into the belly of the gorge.

At one point, the narrow walls prevented Aaron from maneuver-ing the chopper into a good viewing position, so he asked me to hang out the side to look at an interesting fissure below. I looked over at Larry. His expression said, *Better you than me, pal.*

I extended the seat belt as far as it would go, then wrapped the metal tongue with electrical tape so that it wouldn't release acci-dentally. With my heart hammering in my ears, I stepped one foot out on the skids, fighting the icy gusts and trying to keep my bal-ance under the tremendous blast of the rotors. I craned my neck as far as I could, gripping the door housing with frozen fingers as I peered straight down.

Empty.

No ark, no shattered hull, no pieces of boat floating down the ravine.

I could see how, from much greater distances, others might have mistaken the huge fragments of rock we saw for the chiseled hull of a ship or the striations of petrified wood. Knowing that it might be our last chance, we kept searching the Ahora Gorge, revisiting every crag and crevasse and hoping that we might make a sighting.

I wanted, *needed,* to see something. But the sad fact remained that despite the provocative stone shapes, the canyon appeared to be bare of human artifacts.

Aaron pointed to a protrusion of rock on the western slope that interested him. It rested at about 14,500 feet. It looked like a big rock to me, but one year later, Chuck Aaron would return to that site by helicopter and proclaim the blackened, snow-encrusted protrusion to be Noah's ark. The newspapers would report it and spread the word around the world. Later, he said that he had been mistaken and that it was only rock. I deeply respect Aaron, and I wonder if he may have had a jolt of ark fever.

We left the gorge and canvassed the entire mountain for as long as our fuel held out, cataloging questionable landmarks and eyeing each ice cap and formation from different heights and angles. We were determined to leave no slope, rock pattern, or crevasse unexplored. In a single afternoon, we inspected every viable geologic anomaly cited by dozens of eyewitnesses, but we saw no ark, no boat, no wood, and nothing else of interest.

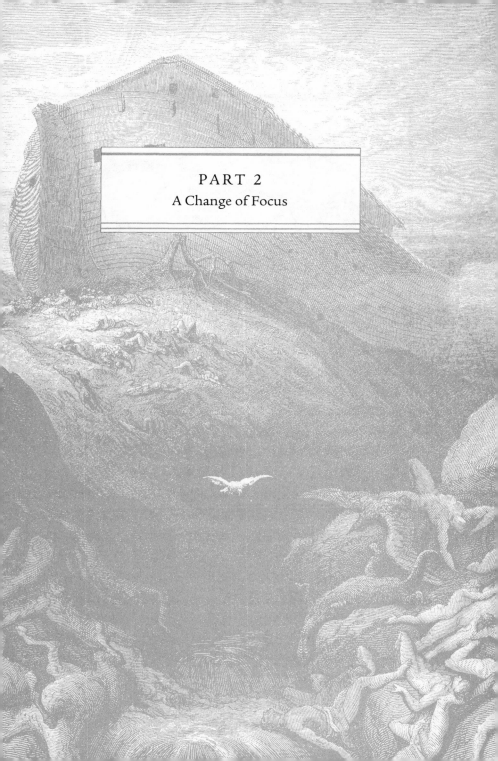

PART 2
A Change of Focus

Map of the "Terrestrial Paradise," showing Noah's Ark below the Caspian Sea on the Summit of "Mont Ararat." Pierre Daniel Huet's conception from Calmet's *Dictionnaire historique del la Bible* (1722).

CHAPTER 5

THE PHONE CALL

Colorado Springs, September 1998

Ten years passed before I gave the search for Noah's ark any more serious thought. Other adventures beckoned, including two clandestine trips into Saudi Arabia to search for the real Mount Sinai and several trips to Israel, Egypt, and Ethiopia, following the trail of the Ark of the Covenant. I've told the story of these expeditions in my book *Relic Quest*.

One evening in 1998, I received a call at my office in Colorado Springs. An elderly gentleman named Phil Burman wanted to talk about Noah's ark. After a brief introduction, this retired engineer shared his opinions about the ark's possible location.

"You're all looking for Noah's ark in the wrong place," he declared. "It *can't* be on Mount Ararat in Turkey."

His manner hit me the wrong way, reminding me of countless calls I had fielded from an assortment of strange people over the years—the kind of people who are so invested in their theories and speculations that they won't listen to any contrary evidence but are determined to drag you over to their side of the argument. I tried to extract myself from the phone call, politely reminding Mr. Burman that others had proposed such a possibility. I also explained that I had moved on to other things, but he refused to quit talking. He pushed ahead, saying that he had read about me in a magazine article that discussed my search in Saudi Arabia for the real Mount Sinai. He said that he admired the way I had trusted the Bible to lead us through the desert on that search. I thanked him and prepared to hang up, but again he resisted.

"Read Genesis 11:1-2," he barked. I hesitated but grudgingly obliged, curious to see how he might bend Scripture to serve his cause. I had skimmed these verses a hundred times. They detail the years after the Flood when Noah's ancestors migrated into neighboring lands to repopulate the earth. "Read it out loud," he pressed. I recited the passage, hoping to humor him.

"Now the whole earth had one language and one speech. And it came to pass, as they [the clans of Noah's sons] journeyed from the east, that they found a plain in the land of Shinar, and they dwelt there." Before I could continue, Burman interrupted. "There! Now back up and tell me what that phrase 'journeyed from the east to find a plain in the land of Shinar' means."

I didn't catch his drift. "Don't you see?" he persisted. "The verse proves that the ark couldn't be on Mount Ararat—or anywhere in Turkey, for that matter."

"Why?" I asked, still scratching my head. Burman explained

that the passage offered a rare fixed point from which to determine the ark's approximate landing site. After the Flood, Noah's descendants branched out, moving westward into the land of Shinar. And where is Shinar? Experts widely identify it as ancient Babylonia, in the heartland of the Mesopotamian Valley, in present-day Iraq. The city of Babylon stood near what is now Baghdad.

"Look at any map," he insisted. "Mount Ararat lies due north of Iraq—not to the east."

He was right. The biblical evidence did seem to indicate that the ark could not have landed in Turkey.

"Case closed!" Burman snapped. "If you believe the Bible, then the passage eliminates the possibility that either the ark or Noah's family could have landed in Turkey."

He now had my full attention, and the implications of his argument intrigued me. If Noah's descendants now lived somewhere east of Shinar—in other words, east of modern-day Iraq, that could only mean that Noah and his family had lived in Iran or somewhere beyond it, such as Afghanistan or India. They came from somewhere in the east and migrated west into Shinar. Such a solid, plausible clue sheds light on why no one has ever found the ark on Mount Ararat. On the weight of Phil Burman's words, I could see the rationale for eliminating Turkey altogether as a place to look for the ark.

"But if the ark can't be found in Turkey," I asked, "where is it?"

"That's not my problem," he said. "I simply called to alert you to what the Bible says. Now it's up to you or someone else who believes the Bible to do your homework and find it."

It was an unsubtle dare. I took it as such and thanked him for the call, assuring him that I would look into the matter. But as I put the phone down, a torrent of doubt crashed in on me. "Everyone knows the ark landed on Mount Ararat," I whispered to the empty room, "and Mount Ararat is in Turkey."

As the days passed, I couldn't get the conversation out of my mind. I inspected some old maps and verified Burman's claim about Shinar—it did lie in the area of Babylonia. Modern scholars identify Shinar as a region in present-day Iraq; the *New Bible Dictionary* defines Shinar as "the land in which were situated the great cities of Babylon."[1] The Bible states that the first cities of the kingdom of Nimrod (Noah's great-grandson) included "Babylon, Erech, Akkad and Calneh, in Shinar" (Genesis 10:10, NIV). So it appeared that Noah's descendants really had migrated from the east into the region now known as Iraq.

But then I encountered a roadblock, an apparent problem with Phil Burman's interpretation of Genesis 11:2. When I compared different translations of the Bible, I discovered a discrepancy. The New King James Version, the translation I was using, says "they journeyed from the east," which supported Burman's case; but the New International Version says, "As men moved eastward," which would mean that the mountains of Ararat were *west* of Shinar rather than east. In a margin note, the NIV also offers two alternate readings, "from the east" and "in the east." So which translation is the more accurate one?

To answer that question, I wrote a letter to Dr. Roy Knuteson, an expert in New Testament Greek. He wrote back and explained, "The Septuagint translation of the Hebrew Bible into Greek in 250 B.C. reads 'from the east,' [which is] significant since the Greek-speaking Hebrews knew the exact equivalent of the Hebrew into the Greek, and chose a preposition (*apo*), which means 'from'—not 'in,' or 'toward,' or 'eastward.'" The New King James translation, "from the east," then, is correct, and is consistent with locating the mountain of the ark east of Babylon (Shinar).

LOOKING FARTHER EAST FOR ARARAT

Even after I had satisfied myself that the ark had to have landed somewhere east of Iraq, I wondered how to proceed with my quest to find it. Delving into history and the Bible set my new course of investigation. After hundreds of false sightings on Mount Ararat's slopes, it was time to rethink the traditional understanding of the ark's location. To do so, I had to tune out the usual ark-fevered voices. It wasn't long before I came back around to the one ark "eyewitness" whose story had intrigued me for years: Ed Davis. Had he gazed upon the rotting timbers of the real McCoy, or was he the ultimate victim of ark fever? And whatever he saw, what mountain was he on when he saw it?

In the end, I couldn't dismiss Davis's testimony as simply ark fever. After all, I was sitting right next to the guy when he passed the lie detector test. But neither could I accept it lock, stock, and barrel. I needed to review the facts and resolve whether or not to go looking for Davis's object.

Unfortunately, I'd heard that Ed Davis was in failing health, so any opportunity to glean further information from him was probably lost. Nevertheless, he had given us enough details to support the view that the mountain he thought was Ararat was not the traditional Mount Ararat in Turkey but another large mountain, located somewhere in Iran.

THE POWER OF TRADITION

In the following days, I phoned some friends who had invested a lot of time and resources in searching for the ark in Turkey. When I casually asked, "Now, remind me . . . why are we looking for the ark in Turkey?" the unanimous response came back: "Because that's where Mount Ararat is."

Then I mentioned Genesis 11:2 and noted the pertinent compass headings for Shinar and Babylon. My friends responded with silence. No one wanted to explore this detour. I listened quietly as they admonished me against chasing pipe dreams and listening to crackpots armed with Bible verses, and as they peppered me with accounts of the eyewitnesses "who've seen the ark on Ararat."

The many "eyewitness" accounts tied to the mountain have spawned a cultish mythology among ark searchers. One mysterious report leads to another, and then another, until everyone accepts on faith that the ark sits there, just waiting for someone to discover it. According to ark scholar Lee Spencer, "The story of Noah and the ark is so well entrenched in Western thought that any mountain found to contain the ark is going to be called 'Mount Ararat' by definition."[2]

Bill Crouse—longtime ark searcher, founder of Christian Information Ministries, and author of the well-regarded *Ararat Report*— writes, "If it were not for these [alleged eyewitnesses], it is doubtful that a search would ever have taken place on the mountain the Turks call Agri Dagi and the Armenians call Masis."[3] Crouse has plenty of company in rejecting these accounts as grossly contradictory or of suspect origin. He charitably allows that most sightings (and the amateurish photos supporting them) can be explained by the peak's high composition of large, angular blocks of basalt, which easily create an optical illusion of "huge, ark-like barges." I came to the same conclusion after a close-up view of the Ahora Gorge. Its flinty, angular boulders, sculpted by wind and ice, transform themselves into shapes that mimic the prow of a ship.

Prejudices die hard. It's human nature to want other people to confirm our opinions rather than to test new theories. Though I initially doubted Phil Burman's observations, he opened my eyes to a new paradigm that motivated a lot of new research. His call drove me to the library, where I picked through scholarly old Hebrew texts and esoteric writings on Iran and Iraq.

I learned that it was only in relatively recent times—certainly many centuries after Moses wrote Genesis—that someone had linked the name *Ararat* with the Turkish mountain. Moses wrote Genesis around 1450 BC, at a time when *Ararat* simply denoted a broad region north of Assyria (the upper Mesopotamian Valley).

DEEPER INTO THE PAST

As I pieced the bits together from an odd array of historical texts, a mottled portrait began to emerge of a much older society, established long before anyone uttered the word *Ararat*. I found, for instance, that *Ararat* was an almost arbitrary by-product of a twisted linguistic evolution that grew out of another, far older term. Taken back to its earliest root, *Ararat* sprang from a Hebrew word referred to in Assyrian records as *Urartu*. Bill Crouse explains that the original Hebrew term for the mountains where the ark landed was not, in fact, *Ararat*, but simply *rrt*. In ancient Hebrew, they did not write out the vowels, only the consonants. Later scribes added the vowel "pointings" we see today. Over time, *rrt* evolved into *Ararat* because both words—*Urartu* and *Ararat*—share the same consonants; only

the vowels have changed. Urartu, then, is the true Asiatic forerun-
ner to Ararat/Armenia, a one-time powerful kingdom centered
around Lake Van in southeastern Turkey (near Mount Ararat). David Rohl would later claim in his book *Legend: The Genesis of Civilization, A Test of Time* that "prior to Shalmaneser I's campaign in 1274
B.C., the land Urartu was located in the mountains and plains to the
south of Lake Urmia."[4] This would mean that the region of Ararat,
at its earliest date, was located in Iran, long before it migrated to
the Lake Van area in Turkey.

With the rise of kingdoms and the tumult of wars, Ararat's borders fluctuated, at times extending well into modern-day northern
Iraq, northwestern Iran, eastern Turkey, and the southern reaches
of the Republic of Georgia—quite a broad landscape from which to
mine clues to the ark's fate. With little effort, I stumbled upon preliminary leads that pointed me in new directions. A juicy detective
story had fallen into my lap, and nothing excites me more than
solving a good mystery.

With each new fact, the ark loomed larger, sturdier, and more
real than ever. I was soon in the grip of a new case of ark fever, walking an ancient trail of discovery into the Ararat of long ago, veering
far from the famous mountain in eastern Turkey.

CHAPTER 6
REMAPPING THE SEARCH

I knew as well as anyone about the dozens of ark expeditions that combed the traditional Mount Ararat during the twentieth century. Explorers had used every means available—ground expeditions, helicopter flights to the summit, aerial mapping and photos taken at low elevations, high-resolution satellite imagery, and even ground-penetrating radar—and yet nothing conclusive had ever been found. Given its estimated size—longer than a football field and three stories high—if the ark still exists, it seems incredible that no one has found it. Why have so many supposed eyewitnesses failed to bring back a shred of conclusive evidence?

The Bible tells us that "the ark rested in the seventh month, the seventeenth day of the month, on the mountains of Ararat" (Genesis 8:4), but that it took almost two-and-a-half months for the floodwaters to recede enough for the tops of nearby mountains to break the surface: "The waters decreased continually until the tenth month. In the tenth month, on the first day of the month, the tops of the mountains were seen" (Genesis 8:5). This would seem to indicate that the mountain where the ark came to rest was the tallest for some distance. Because the 17,000-foot Mount Ararat looms higher than any peak in a region extending into the Caucasus Mountains to the north, the Taurus Mountains to the west, the Zagros Mountains to the south, and the ancient Elburz range to the southeast, it rightly became a prime candidate. But there are some problems with settling on Mount Ararat as the most likely location for the ark.

Bill Crouse, of *The Ararat Report,* observes that "for a mountain that supposedly rose from the depths of the Great Flood, there seems to be an almost complete lack of evidence that the mountain was ever underwater."[1] He notes that there should be missing fossil records and deficient layers of sedimentation if the peak sat for even a brief time beneath the waves. The mountain's characteristics instead suggest that it is an extinct volcano. Crouse believes that Ararat's geologic features probably formed during an enormous volcanic eruption centuries *after* the Flood.

Another reason to question whether Mount Ararat is a viable location for the ark to rest is the mountain's relative isolation in the middle of the Anatolian Plain of eastern Turkey. In his 1877 meditation on Mount Ararat, titled *Transcaucasia and Ararat,* James Bryce observes, "There can be but few other places in the world where so lofty a peak (17,000 feet) soars so suddenly from a plain so low, 200 to 3000 feet above the sea, and consequently few views equally grand. . . . Here in Armenia, the mountain raised itself, solitary and solemn, out of a wide, sea-like plain."[2]

A quick check told me that the Bible never mentions Mount Ararat. Instead, Genesis 8:4 says that the ark came to rest "on the mountains of Ararat." Plural. Somewhere in history, someone made a broad leap and interpreted the verse to mean the singular Mount Ararat. The only mountain by that name lies in eastern Turkey, so naturally that's where people thought the ark must be. I was embarrassed to think that we had all been reading the verse selectively, twisting "mountains" into "Mount" and leaning on unverifiable reports to make our case. Ararat, it seems, had been lost in time and no one knew for sure where it was.

What once seemed enigmatic now seemed logical. No one had found the ark because they were looking for it in the wrong place. Not surprisingly, many who had the most to gain from a sincere reading of the Flood account had either misread or carelessly ignored the biblical clues. I knew from tracking the location of Mount Sinai across Egypt and Saudi Arabia that I could trust the Bible's accuracy, yet I had seen respected scholars blindly trust in tradition rather than Scripture to interpret history. I no longer wanted to do this. Phil Burman had caught my attention.

Today, when I read in the Bible that the ark landed in the "mountains of Ararat," I believe it. The isolated twin volcanic cones of the traditional Mount Ararat no longer qualify, in my opinion.

Until Phil Burman's phone call, I had given up hope that the ark existed anywhere. I thought that either the elements had consumed it, or survivors had dismantled it over time for firewood and building materials. Now, other possibilities began to suggest themselves. I tended to agree with Bill Crouse's assertion that "from the perspective of history, there seem to be compelling ancient sources which argue for another site as the final berth of Noah's ark,"[3] but I still had more questions than answers, and my nascent intuitions needed to be developed. I had tracked some faint footprints and stumbled onto a couple of enticing nuggets—new, unmistakable clues pointing to mountains other than traditional Ararat as the ark's location—but I still didn't know where the evidence would lead me.

REEXAMINING ED DAVIS'S STORY

On my three trips to Turkey, I had tried to align details of Ed Davis's account with what I could observe on Mount Ararat, but the prominent features we noted while flying in Chuck Aaron's chopper—ridges, rocks, canyons—never jibed with Davis's descriptions. He had seen sizable rivers rushing down the mountain in wide, roaring channels, but as anyone who has climbed Mount Ararat knows, it lacks even a single river. Even in years of heavy snowmelt its volcanic substrata drink the excess runoff, leaving only a few wispy streamlets.

Davis had also failed to note Mount Ararat's massive ice fields. "Nope, didn't see those," he told me. The distinctive rock formations and trail routes he described (and later meticulously re-created in a hand-drawn topographical map) seemed to belong to another peak altogether. Davis's accounts clashed with other so-called eyewitnesses on such points as the angle of the ark to the peak and its relationship to the surrounding terrain. I found it astonishing that others were able to read enough similarities into Davis's stories to maintain their interest in Mount Ararat.

Privately, I think I always knew that Davis's mountain didn't conform to the Turkish Agri Dagi, yet I rationalized this, nodding along with those who blamed his advanced age and spotty memory for the discrepancies. Who was I to challenge the Ararat experts who had made multiple trips to the mountain and knew its secret recesses by heart? Still, hard as I tried, I could never line up Davis's story with the features of Mount Ararat in Turkey.

I dug up some old videotapes of Ed Davis being interviewed that I had stored in my supply closet. Had I missed something in those early recordings? Did his marathon monologues contain hidden clues that might shed light on my search? I popped a tape in the VCR and within minutes had validated my intuition. Important clues whispered to me from the spaces between his words, guiding me forward like tiny bread crumbs on a winding trail.

On the first tape, Davis was relaxed, sitting at home in his big easy chair. He began by telling how the army had stationed him in Hamadan, Iran, building roads with the Army Corps of Engineers. He reminisced about his Iranian driver, Badi, who first alerted him to the existence of the ark. While loading rocks on a truck at a Hamadan quarry, he said that Badi casually pointed toward a huge mountain range towering far in the distance and said, "That's where my grandfather found the ark."

I tried to listen and watch as if I had never heard Davis's story, and I found the technique enlightening. When he recounted the road trip he and Badi took to find the ark, he said that they drove from Hamadan through Cazbeen and arrived at his father Abas's village (situated near the base of the mountain) within an eight-hour drive. Trundling 500 miles through the mountains, over rugged roads, to get to Ararat in Turkey would have been impossible. I pulled out a map of the region and noted a handful of mountains (some of them of requisite size and elevation) situated within striking distance of Hamadan. All lay well within Iran's borders.

Even without Ed Davis's testimony, Mount Ararat in Turkey had expired in my mind and hopes as the resting place of the ark. My observations sent me back to the library, searching through old tomes on the ancient lands of Assyria, studying maps on the Mesopotamian Valley, and grabbing anything I could find on the long-lost kingdoms of Armenia. Cross-referencing these texts with early Bible translations, I stumbled upon what I thought might be the earliest literary reference to the landing of Noah's ark on Mount Ararat in Turkey—William of Rubruck's thirteenth-century travelogue, *The Journey of William Rubruck to the Eastern Parts of the World, 1253-1255*. In it, Rubruck chronicles an Armenian folk tradition that Noah's ark had settled on Mount Masis (the Armenian name for Agri Dagi, or Mount Ararat).

But then I found a much earlier account, written by Faustus of Byzantium in the fourth century AD, nine hundred years prior to Rubruck. Faustus used the term *Mount Ararat* to refer to a specific mountain—rather than a region—as the landing place of the ark.

What is interesting about these otherwise nearly identical accounts is that in his fourth-century essay, Faustus located the ark incident on Mount Ararat, but not in Turkey. His Ararat lay hundreds of miles south in the Gordyaen Mountains along Iraq's northern border. In his later version, Rubruck made a drastic leap, perhaps by mistake, in transporting the entire event to Turkey's Mount Ararat.

Each little clue that emerged pulled me farther from Turkey. Though the Bible doesn't tell us exactly where the ark is located, it provides plenty of clues that limit the search. As the clues add up, it appears more logical to pursue a landing site in Iran or points far-ther east.

Reviewing the Ed Davis tapes, I sensed that if he hadn't seen the actual ark, he had seen a convincing large object in Iran that he be-lieved with all his heart was the ark. In any event, I wanted to find out what he had actually seen. I hoped that I could solve the mys-tery as if it were a police investigation. The hunt for the ancient ark had now intersected with clues from the Bible and Ed Davis's in-credible story.

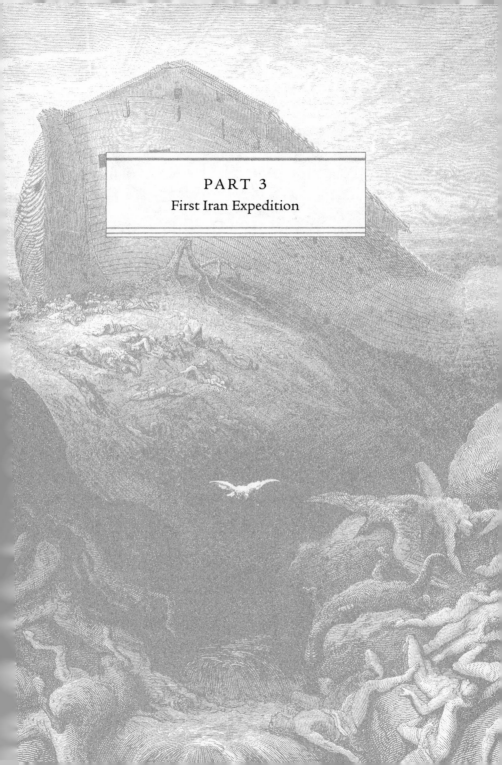

PART 3
First Iran Expedition

Map of Armenia showing "Ararat Mons" (Mountains in Region of Iran) from *Petras Plantius 1552 & 1622.*

CHAPTER 7
EAST OF SHINAR

Tehran, November 1998

"Why don't you just go for it?"

"What?"

I didn't expect to hear those words from my wife, Terry. So I said it again. "Did you hear me? I said I'm thinking of going to Iran to do research on Noah's ark."

"I heard you, Bob," she said, her eyes showing quiet resignation. "You know I'm not keen on your going to Iran, but I have watched you work hard on this project for several years, and if you think the ark is there, go for it."

Terry is my best friend. She has been my greatest supporter since the day I formed the Bible Archaeology Search and Exploration (BASE) Institute and embarked on this wild career. She has demonstrated a saintly patience and a cheerful heart as I've traveled all over the world in search of biblical artifacts. She has been my confidante and sounding board, a wonderful listener. She has provided a steady voice of reason in moments of doubt, and she never hesitates to voice stern words of caution in the face of my crazy schemes. I have trusted her instincts and more than once backed off a dangerous project when she expressed grave concerns.

So when she said I was free to go to Iran, I was certain that I had heard wrong. Didn't she know that Iran regards the United States as the "Great Satan"? A travel advisory, in effect for more than two decades, warns Americans against even the thought of visiting the Islamic Republic of Iran. And for good reason—the Iran hostage crisis seems like only yesterday.

As I recall, Iranian militants seized the U.S. Embassy in Tehran in 1979 when the Shah of Iran was admitted into the United States for medical treatment. They took sixty-six Americans hostage, promising their release if the United States returned the Shah to stand trial. President Carter refused and struck back with economic sanctions. When the militants finally released their prisoners in January 1981—444 days later—it marked the start of a long, ugly season of self-defeating relations between the two countries.

In the hearts and minds of many Iranians, we committed the unforgivable sin of supporting the late Shah and his hated Pahlavi regime, blamed for one of the worst cycles of poverty, joblessness, and repression in Iran's history. While the Shah and his inner circle enriched themselves on petrodollars, the masses suffered from runaway inflation and the abuse of the Shah's SAVAK security force, which killed thousands of demonstrators in the streets of Tehran.

America added insult to injury by supporting Iraq in the bloody

Iran-Iraq War of 1980–88, in which Iraq used poison gas to invade Iran's oil-rich Khuzestan province. Things worsened when the United States shot down an unarmed Iranian jetliner over the Persian Gulf in 1988.

The domestic chaos created by Ayatollah Khomeini's regime prompted Iran to turn increasingly inward and become hostile toward outsiders. Following the Ayatollah's death in 1989, a shaky economy crippled the country, while the Persian Gulf War further exacerbated anti-Western animosities. Today, Iran finds itself ostracized by the international community for its complicity with violent terrorist groups such as the Hezbollah and the Iranian Revolutionary Guard, each responsible for a series of bloody bombings and kidnappings around the globe.

Given this sordid past, I could hardly have picked a more threatening environment in which to continue my search for the ark. Two decades after the hostage crisis, Iran remained one of the most fearsome places on earth for a traveling American. Yet I felt I had to take the risk.

I made a quick mental note of the pros and cons of blitzing Iran. On the pro side, it's cheap to travel there. If I could swing a visa, it meant taking one week of my life to have a fun adventure, see some exotic new sights, and maybe even catch a drift of the ark. In the best-case scenario, everything would go smoothly and I would make the discovery of the ages. At worst, I could be arrested, tossed in jail, or killed.

I calculated five to three in favor of going.

IRAN OR BUST

Initial efforts brought no encouragement. I kept slamming my head into the same brick wall of bureaucratic doublespeak that I had encountered when trying to enter Saudi Arabia. The more foreign consulates and travel consultants I spoke with, the less likely it appeared that I would get a visa. As if reading from identical press releases, they all agreed that "Americans are not traveling in Iran!"

Next, I checked off a very short list of contacts that might have the connections to pull a few strings. I called on a Jewish attorney I knew in New York City. He had sought me out on the Mount Sinai question and once mentioned that some clients of his were strategically employed at five travel agencies in the Big Apple. None proved much help; each was incredulous that I wanted to visit Iran, and each recited the standard, brusque refrain: "Americans are not traveling in Iran."

Now I began to worry. I needed a breakthrough while I still had the nerve to go. It didn't take long to realize that I would have to pull the strings myself. I asked the attorney to fax me the Yellow Pages listing all the New York City travel companies and quickly found several listings for Iranian agencies. None of them wanted to help a non-Iranian from Colorado travel to a country where he might get shot.

Finally, I called Unique Travel, and a woman named Nahid answered the phone. I asked her about a visa.

"Yes, I can do that," she replied without hesitation. It happened that her Jewish relatives still lived in Iran, part of a shrinking but still sizable Jewish population active in bazaar and jewelry trade in the cities of Tehran, Hamadan, Shiraz, and Esfahan.

"We're all descendants of the Jerusalem Jews," Nahid said. When I didn't make the connection, she clarified, "You know, the Jews taken captive in Jerusalem by Nebuchadnezzar, and sent to live as exiles in Persia during the time of Esther and Mordecai" (Esther 2:5-7).

Descendants of Esther and Mordecai in Iran? I hadn't considered that, but it pleased me to be reminded of the eminent role that Persia had played in Old Testament events. Nahid was a godsend. She lined up my visa in no time—a few faxes sent back and forth to her Jewish cousins did the trick. Then she located a guide familiar with the terrain and friendly to my cause. My spirits soared; I set a departure date, reserved my plane tickets, and began planning my itinerary.

THE ZAGROS MOUNTAINS

I narrowed my search to the Zagros Mountains, a rugged range straddling the Iraqi/Iranian border in an area that fit the general biblical description, "east of Shinar." The Zagros range sits due east of Baghdad, running southeast to northwest from the Persian Gulf to southeastern Turkey. It seemed a logical place to start.

Phil Burman disagreed. He believed that the mountains of Ararat lay much farther east, perhaps into Afghanistan, or even the high mountains of Tibet, but those sites never made sense to me. They were far away from Urartu, and the Flood's survivors would have had to cross Iran's deadly Dasht-e Kavir Desert, one of the most inhospitable places on earth. It is an arid, salty wasteland so vast and hot that ancient populations avoided it completely. I was convinced that the real mountains of Ararat lay "east of Shinar" but not east of the Dasht-e Kavir. Even Cyrus the Great in the sixth century BC, leading his great army west from Persia to attack Babylon, had to zigzag east through the Zagros along the Diyala River to reach his adversary.[1]

I settled the matter in my mind. What harm could come from flying into Tehran, hiring a guide, driving to the southeast rim of the Zagros Mountains, and poking around? I would simply ask the locals if anyone had heard of Noah's ark. Maybe I could look in museums and check the local libraries, or perhaps I would get lucky and find some other clue. If local traditions of the ark existed, it shouldn't take long to uncover them. Possibly I would even find that mountain from which Ed Davis had gazed down into a high rocky canyon at a large wooden barge on an icy precipice.

With a tourist visa in my vest and a lump in my throat, I hopped a plane for Tehran. It was October 1998, just a few weeks before Ed Davis died.

INTO PERSIA

Besides the clues contained in Scripture, other fascinating facts supported the idea that Noah and his family settled in Persia following the great Flood and then fanned out into surrounding lands to rebuild the human race.

The oldest known written language, Proto-Elamite, originated in Iran, taking its name from Elam, Noah's grandson, who may have founded the Elamite Empire in southwestern Iran.[2] The world's oldest-known pottery was unearthed in the dusty plains west of the Dasht-e Kavir Desert. Iran has 129 species of mammals, a number nearly equal to that of all Europe, which is four times larger and much more varied ecologically. Iran has 450 species of birds and 250 species of lizards; with its other wildlife, Iran is one of the most diverse areas of animal life on the planet.[3] It may be where grain was first cultivated and animals were domesticated. These facts suggest that Iran may have been the cradle of life for modern civilization following the devastating global flood.

Though such speculations are interesting, they quickly fade when a newcomer lands in teeming, sooty Tehran. From the airplane window, while circling Tehran's international airport, Iran looks like any other densely populated society around the globe. Upon landing, passengers are funneled into a great gray cinderblock structure devoid of charm or warmth, its corridors crawling with more armed guards than any place I have ever visited. I deplaned in late afternoon, took a deep breath, and found myself running a gauntlet of security checkpoints.

Since my exploits in Saudi Arabia, I had learned to dread this compulsory rite of travel in the Middle East. As I approached the first checkpoint, an Iranian security guard eyed me with disdain. *What's he looking at?* I wondered. My imagination had some frightening ideas that I did my best to ignore.

Handing the customs officer my visa and passport, I braced myself for the worst, knowing the nightmarish ordeal of having one's documents and bags pored over in countries hostile to the United States. Enduring the scrutiny of clench-jawed young officers trained in the art of making you sweat becomes a tense, aggressive rite. They searched my eyes for the least sign of strain and then tapped their computer keyboards with such urgent speed that I imagined my smallest childhood indiscretions popping up on the monitor. The young officer stopped typing, calmly handed back my visa, and motioned me on to baggage claim.

Outside the terminal, I searched for my guide, picturing a stocky, bearded Iranian with one tooth and a patch over his eye, probably named Ali. Nahid had said that the guide would meet me in the waiting area. A huge crowd milled about, with dozens calling out and waving signs with people's names. I finally saw my name on a dainty placard toward the back. It was held by a woman in full Iranian raiment.

I hadn't expected a woman.

I looked her over for a moment. Young and petite, arrayed in customary dark head-scarf, she wore the traditional black chador—the loose, flowing cloak that covers Iranian women from head to ankle. I raised a hand and she approached.

"Mr. Bob, hello, my name is Fatima. Welcome to Tehran. I am your guide."

I blurted out something idiotic like, "Oh—you're a woman." A clumsy start that I was certain must have offended her.

She replied graciously. "I'm sorry you are disappointed. But I am your appointed guide. If you have all your bags, we shall go. You will rest tonight, and tomorrow we will tour Tehran. The next day we leave for Ahvaz."

Though touring Iran with a woman didn't seem like a good idea, I soon warmed to it. Fatima's English was flawless, she was friendly, and under her scarf I saw kind, pleasant eyes. I guessed that she was about thirty years old. I reached out to shake her hand in apology for my awkward greeting, but she pulled back.

"No, I'm sorry," she said. "It is not allowed."

I had a world of things to learn about Iranian etiquette, a problem that would be greatly complicated by having a female guide. I knew, for instance, that men cannot even sit next to a woman in Iran unless specifically invited to do so. Yet here stood Fatima, the lovely, smiling face of Iran to the outside world. She was devoutly Muslim and highly educated—she had two master's degrees, one in engineering. I understood why Iran's travel bureau would pair her with an American tourist. Fatima hailed a taxi, and we sped through Tehran's swarming streets to the stately Grand Azadi Hotel. The next day, we would fly south, where I would begin my search near the Iraqi border.

TO AHVAZ

"Lotfan," said a voice from behind. I turned to see the fully-scarved, black-robed Iranian flight attendant glaring at me. "Please, sir," she continued in halting English, "dat," she pointed at my video camera, "iz note permitted."

I'd taken the opportunity to videotape from my window seat a stretch of the Zagros Mountains 30,000 feet below.

"Oh, beba . . . khshid," I stammered, trying to summon an appropriate Persian phrase but quickly resorting to English. I lifted the small camcorder. "Forgive me. I didn't know."

The stewardess smiled weakly and continued her rounds. I put the camera back in its case and leaned back in my seat.

"What's the big deal?" I whispered to Fatima. "Is it a national secret that Iran has mountains?"

Our Iran Air commuter flight took us south toward Ahvaz, a sprawling industrial city located eighty miles north of the Persian Gulf. Its location on the southwestern flank of the central Zagros Mountains made it the ideal starting point. I already regarded the Zagros, due east of ancient Babylon, as the "mountains of Ararat." They weren't quite the imposing peaks of the Colorado Rockies, but they looked impressive enough from the air. Easily the Middle East's dominant mountain range, they formed an impenetrable curtain between Iran and Iraq and defined Iran's western edge.

As we descended into Ahvaz, the Zagros slowly shrank and flattened into a vast plain of marshy lowlands, sand dunes, and salt lakes that spread south for hundreds of miles toward the gulf. The great Karun River cut through the landscape, bisecting both mountain and plain en route to the sea. For thousands of years, the Karun has provided a narrow gateway to Iran's interior, carving a meandering pass through the mountains and linking the Persian Gulf with the southern mainland.

The plane tilted into landing position. Fatima leaned over and traced a line on the window with her finger, from Ahvaz south to the Persian Gulf, then west to the Iranian-Iraqi frontier.

"See the triangle?" she asked. "That's where southwestern Iran meets the great Mesopotamian Valley, just east of where the Tigris and Euphrates rivers come together."

Ah, I thought. *The land of Shinar.*

Landing at Ahvaz's unremarkable Kheyaun-e Zeitun Airport, we found our driver, a real-life Ali, waiting for us at the gate. His appearance perfectly fit the stereotype I had imagined of a toothless, bearded guide. If Ali seemed rather humorless and gruff, his punctuality more than made up for it. He seemed like someone we could depend on.

Heeding to Fatima's orders, Ali packed us into his forest-green Peugeot and chauffeured us toward downtown Ahvaz. The road into town was bounded on all sides by rhythmically pumping oil wells, greasy oil storage facilities, and immense, smoke-belching refineries like those I had seen in central Texas. This was the fertile crescent of Iran's petroleum industry, and a quick surveillance told me why, a mere decade earlier, Ahvaz had stood on the frontline of the Iran-Iraq War.

When Saddam Hussein was the Iraqi premier, he knew what he wanted when he made his 1980 land grab in southern Iran, attacking on the feeble grounds that the oil-rich Khuzestan province was once part of Iraq. Seeing all the refineries, I realized that his motive had been pure greed.

While the war exacted an incalculable toll in lives on both sides, Iran had fought with a vengeance. Badly outgunned and the clear underdog, Iranian troops were possessed by a fierce religious fervor. At the time of the cease-fire in mid-1988, neither side had achieved its objectives. For the first time since WWI, the world witnessed the grisly effects of poison gas and trench warfare.

To my surprise, Ahvaz had a rich biblical history, its origins dating back to the reign of King Darius in the sixth century BC. Many Old Testament events had unfolded nearby, though unremitting Iraqi bombardments and a history of military conquest and subjugation have reduced most of the area's historic past to rubble.

The city resembles a giant war memorial; its prominent thoroughfares are bedecked with solemn murals and oversized statues of martyred soldiers. Throughout Ahvaz, plaques on strategic walls and buildings eulogize the town's anonymous "Brave Ones." Even the city's impressive network of modern suspension bridges are still pitted and cracked from heavy artillery fire.

I took a moment to orient myself geographically. Just a few miles to the south lay Kuwait, and Basra, the base of Iraq's invasion forces, was to the west. I was in the epicenter of some of the most destructive cross-border combat of the past century. Despite the government's valiant campaign to rebuild Ahvaz, the devastation of war remained obvious.

It was dusk when we arrived at our hotel. The Fajr Grand Hotel, on the east bank of the Karun River, was across the street from a rundown amusement park whose Persian-motif carnival rides squeaked and wobbled in comic disrepair. Light bulbs dangled from cords, signs tilted on their hinges, and everything looked like it had come straight from the junkyard.

As I unpacked, the orange glow of the refinery towers blazed like an artificial sunset through my north window. Flames from their spouts leapt hundreds of feet into the air, burning an astounding volume of excess oil and gas.

Sleep came fast, so I was rested and excited the next morning when we drove north toward the southern Zagros. Ali stopped at every little roadside village or market, at my request. At each stop, Fatima asked the assembled onlookers, "Have you heard of Noah's ark?" Invariably, she returned crestfallen.

"I'm sorry, Mr. Bob, but they haven't heard of your ark, either."

CHAPTER 8

A GLIMMER OF HOPE

By late afternoon, we reached Susa, still on the Mesopotamian plain but within easy driving distance of the Zagros foothills. Any Bible student recognizes Susa (*Shush* in Iranian) as one of the great cities of ancient Persia. It is among the oldest cities in the world, its roots extending back to four thousand years before the birth of Christ. Susa's ruins, inscriptions, tombs, and even the dust of its streets are a perpetual link to Scripture's earliest events, perhaps as far back as the great Flood of Noah. Seeing it with my own eyes illuminated a distant past I had been struggling to understand.

Hundreds, even thousands, of old artifacts, consisting mainly of pottery shards from ancient empires litter Susa's burial mounds. Most of them lie scattered in plain view above ground. The mounds are highly prized in archaeological circles, but most Iranians are indifferent to them. Susa's extremely rare bounty of Parthian-era "painted ware"—whose geometric designs of water birds, hunting dogs, ears of corn, horse heads, and palm leaves lay strewn among the half-buried remnants—provides a clear glimpse into the aesthetic tastes of the Elamite culture. I plucked a 4,000-year-old shard from the dirt. Turning it over, I saw four distinct fingerprints fired into its glaze, no doubt belonging to the goblet's potter. It was exciting to think that I might have touched the work of an artisan commissioned by Darius's court.

Strolling the grounds set me to daydreaming, and I imagined the entire region covered by floodwaters, everyone drowned but Noah and his family. As the waters receded and the mountains rose, I saw people migrating down into these ancient plains, building cities and fashioning a culture.

Susa is mentioned repeatedly in Scripture, appearing first in the book of Ezra as the home of the Elamites (Ezra 4:9). The prophet Nehemiah later wrote of carrying on his affairs "in the citadel of Susa" during the time that the Lord inspired him to rebuild Jerusalem (Nehemiah 1:1, NIV). Later still, Esther, Mordecai, and the other exiled Jews regarded Susa as their home when their lives became embroiled in the intrigues of King Xerxes' court. Finally, the prophet Daniel was cloistered in Susa when he received a vision from God: "In my vision I saw myself in the citadel of Susa in the province of Elam" (Daniel 8:2, NIV).

Sadly, since those grand years, Susa's splendor has faded. It was destroyed in 331 BC by Alexander the Great and exists today as little more than a dusty village, with no evidence of its fabled past. Gone are the lavish palaces of Untash Gal or Darius I, a successor to the Nebuchadnezzar who threw Daniel's friends into the fiery furnace

(Daniel 3:19-21). Eventually, Susa's ruins disappeared completely beneath the dusty landscape, resurfacing again only in the mid-1800s when a British archaeologist stumbled upon the site and began to excavate its wonders.

As we entered the city, Fatima remarked, "Mr. Bob, did you know that the prophet Daniel's tomb remains in Susa? Perhaps you would like to see it?"

"Yes, of course I would," I replied, surprised—awestruck really—to learn that the tomb of one of God's greatest prophets could still be seen and visited. Until then, I hadn't fully appreciated the antiquity and historical richness of this dusty plain.

We arrived at Daniel's tomb in the heat of the afternoon. It was housed in a large white building with a domed, sugarloaf tower. The rectangular courtyard was filled to capacity with kneeling Muslims gathered from across Iran. The throng of pilgrims, mostly men, approached the ornately carved, gold-plated crypt with stoic reverence, almost as if the prophet still lived.

"Daniel's bones still lie inside," noted Fatima as we watched the crowd circle the tomb, lost in their meditations. Each person rubbed it affectionately and, in some instances, kissed or pressed their foreheads against it, then rubbed themselves all over as if anointing themselves with invisible oil. The closer one got to the prophet's tomb, apparently, the more potent the blessing. It called to mind other great men of God—Abraham, Moses—revered in both the Christian and the Islamic traditions. Seeing this commotion over Daniel's tomb reminded me of the distant genealogy shared between Christians and Muslims.

As I reflected on the proceedings, Fatima's uncomfortable task continued. As per our agreement, she shuffled glumly about, approaching one pilgrim after another with the question, "Have you heard or seen anything of Noah's ark?" Here, as elsewhere, there were blank stares and cold shoulders; here, as elsewhere, Fatima returned from her chore humiliated, clearly wanting nothing more to do with Noah and his blasted boat.

Ali chauffeured our bone-jarring ascent into the high Zagros. Navigating its terrible folds and crags, I understood why Cyrus and other invaders found this knobby cordillera such an imposing range. In Colorado, modern interstate highways have tamed the Rockies, but no such engineering had yet humbled the Zagros. Here, craggy passes and rutted cart paths ruled.

By mid-afternoon, we had reached an obscure little town known as Khorramabad, at the bottom of a spreading gorge. An impoverished, third-world village, Khorramabad boasts few amenities to soothe the road-weary traveler. Mangy beasts roam the streets, and the town's only hotel features rooms without windows. My room had a square hole in the wall—no air-conditioning—and it smelled. The bathroom was spartan. Outside, a blacksmith ground metal against a sparking stone wheel, confirming my opinion of Khorramabad as a noisy, hot, inhospitable hamlet. I counted it a lackluster honor when the hotel manager told me that no other American had set foot in his hotel.

We stowed our bags and ventured out to mingle with the natives. We had yet to find a single clue of the ark's whereabouts, and my time in Iran was nearing its end. This crude village represented perhaps my last chance to leave the country with an arguable defense for my theory. Needing to motivate Fatima for another round of inquiries, I asked, "Are you ready?" then added, "Time is short, and we have to stay focused."

She didn't bite, but rebelled openly. "Please, Mr. Bob, don't make me ask again. It is no good now. They will just think I'm crazy."

I sensed her pain. Of the close to two hundred people we had surveyed, not one had smiled at her, much less given us a solid lead. For a dainty flower like Fatima, this lengthy record of rejection smelled of disgrace.

We walked to the town square. The outdoor market was pungent with exotic meats and overripe vegetables, combined in a moldering potpourri that drew clouds of flies. Scanning the colorful crowd of shoppers and vendors, I hoped, for Fatima's sake, to single out a friendly face. As we wended our way through the gallery, I finally settled on an old man with a woolly white beard. He stood across the square, leaning casually against a stone arch in the pose of a resident sage. If anyone knew anything of the local legends, I guessed that he might.

"Fatima," I said gently, "see that old man? Go ask him."

Like a scolded child, she exhaled a long, pitiful groan, hunched her shoulders, and shuffled off across the square. I trailed close behind.

As we approached, the old gentleman flashed a grin, eyeing me intently. I thought it a cheery omen, but Fatima had long since run out of smiles. She walked right up and asked him bluntly if he had seen or heard of Noah's ark. The old man's eyes grew large, and he smiled to show us a mouthful of rotten teeth before reeling off a rapid-fire string of sentences. I had no idea what he was saying, but it was the first time someone hadn't mocked or ignored us. He jabbered some more and for a moment I saw Fatima's face go slack. She glanced back at me with round, pensive eyes, then irritably grilled the poor man with a new round of questions, leaning in close to hear his response. He kept grinning and talking and point-ing, and when Fatima finally swung back around, she appeared as if she had seen Daniel's ghost.

"Mr. Bob," she said, "this gentleman says he knows of Noah's ark."

"You're kidding!" I said. "Where?"

"He says it lies between Nahavand and Hamadan, and that it can still be seen today."

"Between Hamadan and Nahavand?" I'd heard of Hamadan—that was where Ed Davis had been stationed. "Where is Nahavand?"

Fatima's droopy countenance lifted, her gloom replaced by a glint of excitement. In a matter of seconds, the heady rush of ad-venture had drawn her in. The old man kept up his breathless com-mentary, as if he had waited years for just this moment.

Fatima translated, slowly and carefully: "He says that after the Flood, the ark of Noah came to rest in the mountains of Nahavand." "*Nahavand* means 'Noah's land.' He says that between Nahavand and Hamadan lies a tall mountain called Sarkashti. He says we will find the ark there."

GETTING THERE

Standing in the teeming market as if alone, we winnowed from the old man a complete list of details and instructions, including a rough map and the name of a driver with a four-wheel-drive vehicle who could take us high into the upper Zagros to Mount Sarkashti. We learned that *Sarkashti* means "the top portion of a ship," evi-dently referring to the ark.

Had we really struck pay dirt? There was only one way to find out. We would drive back down the mountains to Kermanshah, three hours west of Khorramabad, and find our driver. We would spend the night at Kermanshah, rise early, and take the back roads to a secluded town known as Oshtorinan, situated between Hamadan and Nahavand. In between, we would flash by towns and villages whose names I couldn't pronounce or remember—I would leave the details to Fatima. The old fellow insisted that we would find Mount Sarkashti in the heights above Oshtorinan.

And on its summit we would find the ark.

I bristled with excitement, but I also felt wary. It all seemed too simple. Here we were, staking our hopes on the story of a complete stranger who quite possibly made the whole thing up. But then again, in my line of work, one couldn't avoid such risks. I recalled the local bedouin in Saudi Arabia who helped us get our truck out of the sand and pointed us to Mount Sinai. These "happenstance" meetings had always fit my strategy. I had been praying for just such a moment since arriving in Tehran. I thanked the old man and turned to Fatima.

"What's this about a driver with a Land Rover?" I asked. "Where do we find him?"

"The old man says to follow his directions and take the main road to Kermanshah," she said matter-of-factly. "The driver will find us."

Captive now to events beyond my control, I realized that I had neither the time nor the energy to sweat the details, however eccentric they seemed. We retrieved our bags, hopped in Ali's Peugeot and rumbled back down the hogbacks toward Kermanshah. I was exhausted.

In four days, I had traveled more than 1,000 miles across Iran—

roughly the distance from Colorado to California—and had nothing to show for it but a chip of Elamite pottery. As we entered the plain of Kermanshah, thoughts of home filled my mind. After long hours of driving, I was startled to see an older model Land Rover draw alongside us on the gravel road. The driver motioned for us to pull over.

"This is our driver," Fatima said nonchalantly.

How did he recognize us? I wondered. *Had someone called ahead?* It still seemed strange, but this late in a grueling journey, I lacked the energy to question.

I got out of the car and immediately found myself engaged in an awkward haggling session with the owner of the Land Rover, a handsome, sturdy youth with jet-black hair and a chiseled jaw. As always, Fatima translated, informing him of our objective and asking his price. He began carping and quibbling, fussing and flapping his arms before even mentioning a price. He apparently planned to make the very idea of a trip to Oshtorinan seem a fearsome nuisance. He finally motioned that he would simply wash his hands of the whole mess and barked out a Farsi expression meaning, "You can't afford me!"

"How much is he asking?" I inquired of Fatima.

"He wants twenty-five dollars in American currency," she replied.

I almost laughed, reaching for my wallet, but Fatima, embarrassed and insulted by the man's poor manners, took me aside.

"This man is a Lor," she whispered disdainfully. "They are a people who pride themselves on stealing you blind. He will consider it an honor to rob you of as much money as possible."

I looked him over. He owned a Land Rover, which in Iran meant that he was either a gifted businessman or a skillful swindler. I handed him two twenty-dollar bills with instructions to "keep the change." Forty bucks didn't seem too much for asking him to abuse his beautifully maintained SUV. The Lor pocketed the cash, no doubt thinking that he had pulled the biggest heist of the week, and trailed us into Kermanshah.

That night, lying in my hotel bed, I couldn't sleep. To this point, the trip had been a pleasant, mostly calculated tour of some ancient towns and ruins. Now it seemed to be tilting out of my control. I had bought into an old man's story about Noah's ark and had put my life in the hands of a Lorish con man, trusting him to navigate us through a land I would never understand in a hundred years.

MOUNT SARKASHTI

We rose the next morning before sunrise, threw our things into the Land Rover, and began a circuitous, marathon drive into the rugged Zagros highlands. For hours, we climbed into an increasingly austere, scrub-brushed mountain range—8,000 feet, 9,000 feet—bouncing in the back of the SUV and churning up increasingly narrow roads. At midday, we reached the high mountain pass of Mount Sarkashti.

The pass sat in a washboard-ribbed basin, surrounded by high, saddleback ridges ringed in clouds. When our Lorish guide said, "Sarkashti," I took it on faith that he was telling the truth. I still didn't trust him, and the endless climb into increasingly remote mountains had given me ample occasion for paranoia. For all I knew, he had lured us to his mountain lair to set his gang of Lorish bandits on us. I knew that if I disappeared in these canyons, it would be the last anyone would ever hear of me.

"Do you think any other American has ever been through these passes?" I asked Fatima.

"No, Mr. Bob," she said, warily inspecting the premises. "You must be the first."

We stopped at the top of the windblown pass at a roadside stand. The makeshift mud hut was tended by a middle-aged Iranian with an AK-47 slung over his shoulder. The bottles of Fanta soda he sold were chilling in a small brook beside the road. Children appeared and started an impromptu game of tag around the car. Fatima approached the man with the rifle.

"Is this Mount Sarkashti?" she asked. When he nodded affirmation, she proceeded, "Can you tell us where we might find Noah's ark?"

It seemed a silly question, but suddenly another man appeared and shouted gleefully, *"Bale, bale"* (Farsi for "Yes!"). He then pointed skyward to a nearly vertical ridge angling away from the town.

I stared at the steep knoll. "If this is Mount Sarkashti," I said, "then ask him what the ark looks like."

After a quick exchange, Fatima translated the man's vague description. "He calls it big, and square, and . . ." she paused, uncertain of the local slang, "he says it's the color of soil."

I had no idea what that meant, but I began to bounce on my toes, eager to sprint up the mountainside. Trying to remain calm, I asked, "Can he take us there?" After so many years and so many false leads, I could scarcely wait to see what lay over that ridge.

"Yes," Fatima answered. "He says he will take us to it."

THE "COLOR OF SOIL"

Hardly a majestic mountain, Mount Sarkashti stood no more than 11,000 feet high. It struck me as a particularly dreary, desolate butte in a range already poorly vegetated. We set off with the rifle-man in the lead, hiking and, in places, scrambling up the ridge on a slender, hand-hewn trail. In a little over an hour, we reached a broad, downward-sloping plateau with a splendid view of the nearby tablelands. Adrenaline rose in my throat as we crested the last stony crag.

"Where to from here?" I asked, my eyes darting about. Some-thing told me we had a ridge or two yet to climb, as we remained several hundred feet below the summit. But then Fatima said something that shocked me.

"It's here!" she said, pointing to the man with the rifle. "This fel-low says it's here."

"Here? Here where?"

I looked around and saw nothing of interest, and knew by the look on Fatima's face that something was wrong. She pointed to a spot on the ground, forty yards off, and said, "He says it's over there."

I scanned the hillside. I could see no ark. My heart sank. The trickle of adrenaline turned bitter in my throat. Silently, I searched the ground for old pieces of wood, or something—*anything*—to hint of a primitive boat or wooden structure. I found nothing but a massive, sloping indentation in the ground, a sunken hollow of sorts that looked like a shallow crater.

I turned to Fatima. "What's this?" She turned to our host, lifting her arms, bewildered.

The man completely ignored me as he addressed Fatima, her face turning shades of red. She delivered the news, "Mr. Bob, he says this hole . . . is where the ark used to sit."

Ah . . . *the color of soil.* Now it made sense. I stared at the concave depression, trying to visualize a large boat nesting in the cavity. But then I came to my senses.

"Where's the ark?" I wanted to know.

Fatima was flustered, trying to extract information from our now tight-lipped escort. In bits and pieces, she managed to learn that according to local lore, "the ark has been broken apart through the years and has been carted off by the villagers for firewood and to build their homes." Just then two shots rang out, and two AK-47 slugs screamed past my right ear. I stood paralyzed in my tracks.

Slowly, I turned around. Our host stood forty yards off, aiming his AK-47 in my direction. Fatima ran over, holding the hems of her robe in her hands, trying to shield me from his sights. Very calmly, very quietly, she said, "He's very angry and says to go no farther. He says we must go back down the mountain now!"

"Why?" I whispered. "What's the problem? Why can't we be here?"

"He won't say."

Her words were calm but her eyes showed fright. "He says we must go back now."

Hardly the glorious ending I had imagined. Her words left me speechless. I kept staring at our guide in disbelief, but he wouldn't return my gaze. The man with the gun had spoken with two rounds from his rifle. The argument was over.

We began to move down the mountain, a terrible tension in the air. Nothing more was said of the ark. To do so, I feared, would invite disaster. At least the much-anticipated robbery had never happened. Of that I was thankful, but it seemed a small consolation.

Questions hung in the air like a foul odor, and I would probably never know any of the answers. This mountain site was steeped in local tradition as the landing place of the ark. It was a big flat space with a slight depression, and otherwise there was nothing to recommend it. My snooping around had made the man with the gun angry, and he gave no explanation. The mountain had no snow on it at all, so it wasn't Ed Davis's mountain. Ed Davis had clearly described deep snow in the ravines and rocky crevasses on his mountain.

We reached the bottom, and I paid the Fanta salesman a couple of bucks. We returned to the Land Rover and rumbled down the mountain, not bothering to look back. My time in Iran had come to an end. In two days, I would be back in the States, and all I had to show for it was a hole in the ground where the ark was supposed to have been.

"Has anyone else ever been to that site?" I asked Fatima.

She paused and said, "The man on the mountain told me that some Americans in a helicopter once landed there. They worked for an oil company. The man said that they came, landed, looked at the depression, and then left."

I guessed that the men in the helicopter, whoever they were, had heard about the place from locals as the traditional site of the ark just as I had, and had decided to check it out.

I was disappointed as we drove from the mountain, but also encouraged that this part of the Middle East had traditions about the ark. I hoped that other places in Iran might have similar traditions that would propel me closer to an actual site. Was I on to something in Iran, or was I succumbing to ark fever and chasing a ghost that would never be found?

OTHER TRADITIONS

After our misadventures on Mount Sarkashti, we headed north toward Hamadan, meeting other locals who shared hazy stories and distant legends of the ark. They featured the tale of one old man who said he knew of the ark's whereabouts. He agreed to take us there, and after some haggling led us to a nearby mountain the locals consider holy.

"In reverence to the prophet Noah," he said, "Muslims still sacrifice sheep near its summit, which still holds traces of the ark."

When we climbed to the top, we saw nothing but scores of hikers.

As we continued our northern arc toward Tehran, we encountered little bits of regional traditions here and there. It soon became apparent that anecdotes and legends of the ark, the Flood, and Noah abound throughout the central Zagros Mountains.

With each mention of the ark, my mind hearkened back to Ed Davis. Could this be the mountain he climbed? Did Davis drive these roads? Were these rugged Lors of the same tribe that took Davis under their wing? I kept hearing his words, "You'll never believe how big it is!" and envisioned the ark appearing over every other ridge. But it didn't happen on this trip.

I left Iran with the warmest feelings of gratitude toward Fatima and Ali. The trip's results cheered me less, but I resolved to stay the course. It was, after all, only my first foray into Persia. I kept coming back to the central thesis: Iran lies due east of Shinar and remains the most likely region for Ararat.

This would be my sole consolation for the time being.

CHAPTER 9
THE PHOTOS

Colorado Springs, November 1998

It was good to be home in Colorado Springs. I needed time to regroup, take a few weeks off, and rethink my game plan.

Eventually, I went back to the library and immersed myself again in the study of Ancient Persia, Assyria, and the Near East. I piled musty old books on the tables and waded in. It was mind-numbing work, and I soon learned that no one seemed to know for sure the location of ancient Ararat at the time that Genesis was written. The borders had shifted so often, expanding and contracting with time, that it would be impossible to nail down a hard-and-fast location.

The Bible seemed to be a more helpful resource for defining a general region for Ararat. The prophet Jeremiah, circa 630 BC, spoke of Ararat, Minni, and Ashkenaz rallying to battle (Jeremiah 51:27). Although the war itself did not occur until one hundred years later, in 539 BC, when Cyrus the Great of Persia attacked Babylon, the verse supplies a clue to the true region of Ararat, which apparently was located close to Minni and Ashkenaz.

In the *Zondervan Pictorial Encyclopedia of the Bible*, Merrill C. Tenney writes, "Probably Ashkenaz is to be identified with the Scythians, a people who, in the time of Jeremiah, had settled near Lake Urmia, in the region of Ararat (Urartu)."[1] This is a solid clue that Ashkenaz was likely in Iran at the time of Jeremiah. It is more than coincidental that the kingdom of Minni (variously known as Minyas, Minnai, or Mana) arose from the loose unification of several small city-states sitting just south and east of Lake Urmia in present-day northern Iran.[2]

The Bible also refers to Ararat in an account of the assassination of the Assyrian king Sennacherib by his two sons in 681 BC: "Now it came to pass, as he was worshiping in the temple of Nisroch his god, that his sons Adrammelech and Sharezer struck him down with the sword; and they escaped into the land of Ararat" (2 Kings 19:37).

What do we know about the location of this safe haven, where the assassins knew they would receive asylum? The *Jewish Encyclopedia* (1902) tells us that Minni had revolted about the same time as Sennacherib's assassination.[3] If so, it seems logical that to escape punishment the assassins would have fled to their allies near Lake Urmia.

As I studied the Bible with the help of these other resources, my understanding of Ararat was refined, and a picture of the land that Noah once walked gradually emerged. What before had been a vague and confusing concept crystallized into a picture of a mountainous kingdom lying somewhere in northern Iran.

I marked September 6, 1999, on my calendar—the day I would fly to Tehran.

DETOUR TO DOGUBAYAZIT

On August 14, 1999, my friend Dick Bright called from Turkey. "Bob," he said, his voice ebullient, "I think I found it!"

The words didn't register. "Found what?"

"The ark!"

"Where?" I asked.

"The Ahora Gorge," he blurted out, "low into the Abich II Glacier, embedded in the cliff face."

I heard a breathless flutter in his voice, which for the gruff, stoic Dick Bright was wildly out of character. He had been searching for the ark since 1984 and was known in ark circles as "The Bulldog" for his steely determination and stubborn refusal to quit. He had traveled to Turkey about fifteen times and had climbed, flown over, and led enough treks up Ararat to know better than to make such a rash pronouncement. As a former commercial pilot with a doctorate in theology, he could usually be counted on for balance and objectivity. Now, he sounded overconfident.

"I found it, Bob, and I want you to go back up there with me. I have photos; I'll send them to you."

"I don't think so, Dick," I replied, flustered. "I'm getting ready to lead an expedition to Iran in about two weeks, and it doesn't make sense to change course at such a late date."

But he was not to be denied. "Listen, Bob, don't make a decision now. I'm sending the photo to you by Express Mail. Look it over and I'll call you back in a few days." Then he hung up.

When Bright's package arrived on my doorstep, I ripped it open to view his discovery. I was instantly skeptical. The picture was dark and grainy, the detail all but lost in the canyon's bleak shadows. The photo framed a section of fractured rock face overlooking a ledge crammed with boulders. At the center of the ledge was an angular, flint-edged, vaguely boat-shaped object of uncertain size, like hundreds of rocks I've seen on the slopes of Mount Ararat. A closer inspection revealed a boxy boulder with a pointed end—striated here, tapered there—that was little different from dozens of other "mysterious objects" I had seen on film. Knowing the gorge as I did, I thought it was nothing more than a common hunk of basalt with an ice-chiseled, prow-shaped nose.

I studied the picture for a long time, hoping to find some evidence that this might be Noah's ark. It wasn't there. I had to call Bright and give him my honest opinion. "It looks like a fascinating rock with an interesting shape, but that's all."

"I'm telling you, Bob, this is Noah's ark," he insisted. "I saw it with my own eyes. It was just across the Ahora Gorge. I couldn't get to it then, so we need to go back. If you come over, you'll see that we've finally found Noah's ark."

I did not want to return to Mount Ararat. I had been there many times and knew what to expect. The object would turn out to be just another big rock formation or misshapen block of ice, captured through the lens of a camera positioned half a mile away. I had seen variations on this story for years—different people had different photos of different rocks, but the result was always the same. There would be no ark.

Dick Bright, however, was as credible a witness as you could hope to find. He was not a wishful thinker, easily fooled by ark fever. He had looked at this mountain for years and had never before made such a proclamation. I did not want to dismiss his claim, but I remained unconvinced. Ararat's phantom shadows, jutting faults, and fractured, symmetrical joints can fool the most experienced explorer—even Dick Bright with his impeccable credentials. These mirage sightings had been skewing explorers' objectivity for centuries, and a hundred years from now, people will doubtless still be seeing "arks" all over the mountain.

GOING, GOING, GONE

Bright had also called master climber Bob Stuplich and asked, "Do you want to climb the mountain and see the ark?"

It was an unnecessary question: Stuplich would climb an apple crate if you put it in front of him. The higher the mountain, the more dangerous the ascent, the more likely he will be to climb it. Bob is the most capable climber I know.

In the search for Noah's ark, Bob Stuplich, Dick Bright, and I go way back. We are good friends, and when counted together, we have more than forty Middle East ark expeditions among us. We are the old-timers among ark searchers. Bob Stuplich and I are in our early fifties, and Dick Bright says he is in his sixties, but you would never know it—he can out-climb most twenty-year-olds. I had flown around Ararat twice in a helicopter, circled it in a fixed-wing airplane, and logged more research miles in Turkey and Iran than just about anyone, but I had never climbed high on the glacier of Mount Ararat where this object of interest rested.

It was no surprise that Stuplich agreed to join the search. What looks impossible to me is just an interesting challenge to him. He led teams for John Warwick Montgomery in the mid-seventies and for *Apollo 15* astronaut Jim Irwin in the eighties.

As for me, I didn't think Mount Ararat was even the right mountain. My eyes, heart, and mind were now looking to the high mountains of Iran for the landing zone of Noah's lost boat. But because I was in the process of producing a documentary on the various search efforts for Noah's ark, the idea of climbing Mount Ararat was alluring. It would be a chance to get some great shots and show a case of ark fever on film. There was a problem, however. Turkey hadn't issued a climbing permit in more than ten years, and it didn't look as if they would be granting one any time soon. Bright didn't see that as a problem. "You come to Turkey, and I guarantee that we'll have a climbing permit."

He would fulfill that promise, but his getting that permit would almost get us killed.

Dick Bright is a good man. I have known him for a long time and found him to be honest, credible, and reliable. There wasn't the slightest chicanery about his finding, but I knew he had a sweltering case of ark fever. Still, it was too tantalizing an invitation for me to resist. I would go on the expedition, chronicle the search, trail an actual eyewitness who believed he had seen the real ark, and once there we would find little more than snow, ice, and rock—as always. But just maybe, after another failed expedition on Ararat, some ark researcher would glance to the high mountains looming to the east in Iran. Besides, it would be only one extra week of travel, and what's one week?

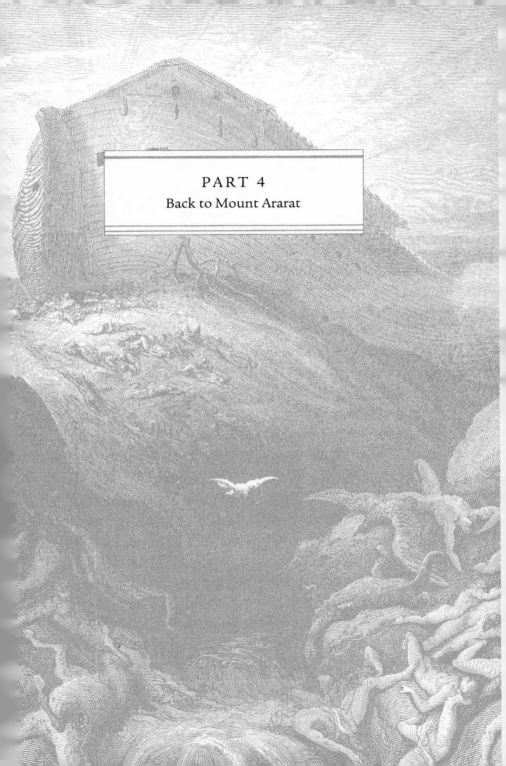

PART 4
Back to Mount Ararat

CHAPTER 10
MEETING THE MOUNTAIN

Turkey, September 1999

The captain's voice boomed over the intercom, and the flight attendants prepared for landing. From my window, the lights of Istanbul glittered like a billion stars off a moonlit sea. I was in Turkey again, and after a domestic flight to Lake Van on the eastern frontier, we met Dick Bright, who awaited us with a confident grin. He herded us into a van, and we drove straight to Dogubayazit, a small, dusty town on Mount Ararat's southern foot. During the drive, Bright said, "Everything's taken care of. I've made all the arrangements."

I understood this as both good news and bad news. We wouldn't have to wait indefinitely for the Turks to grant us permits, but Bright's comment made it clear that nonofficial arrangements were in place. This usually meant a payoff, and that set me on edge—such arrangements had a way of blowing up. I assumed that a sizable gratuity had passed through unofficial channels, most likely through Dick Bright's shrewd, well-connected guide, Micah.

"I just hope this Micah chap puts Bright's 'special arrangement' to good use," I groaned to Stuplich.

"If this plan doesn't work," he whispered back, "we'll have a short, one-way trip up the mountain."

We drove over rutted roads past a waterless wasteland of grimy mud huts, dusty rolling hills, and desolate sheep pastures. Women were in the fields working beneath the blazing sun, some so poor that they didn't even own a sickle for cutting the wheat. Instead, they pulled shafts of grain from the hard clay soil with their bare hands. In every village, little girls mixed sheep dung with straw, patted it into round pies, and stacked it ten feet high next to their homes to use as fuel during the winter.

Three hours into our trip, I could just see the summit of Mount Ararat peeking through the distant haze. The mountain was enormous, but it still seemed an eternity away.

We spent the night in Dogubayazit in clear view of cloud-covered Mount Ararat. I hadn't seen it in more than ten years. With its summit framed by a brooding, rose-peach sunset, it was as proud and as breathtaking as I remembered.

Seated at an outdoor café, we enjoyed a classic Turkish feast of lamb kabobs, vegetables, and rice. Our anticipation of the coming adventure turned the conversation into the testosterone-charged patter of aging men glorying in their most harrowing exploits. The animated dialogue, fueled by our exotic surroundings and spicy fare, set our minds reeling with the agonies and the ecstasies of the painful mountain. Many dashed dreams littered Ararat's slopes, some of my own among them. Although I had never climbed high on the mountain (and therefore slipped low in the table-talk pecking order), I well knew Ararat's reputation as one of the most inhospitable places on earth. Many climbers disappeared up there, swallowed by the many icy crevasses. Of the stout men who made it up and back in one piece, most vowed never to return.

MOUNTAIN MAN

I glanced across the table at Bob Stuplich, the experienced climber and adventurer with whom I had made three previous attempts at Mount Ararat. Tanned, tall, and tawny, Stuplich was a supremely confident man. If anyone could boast self-assurance on the eve of our climb, he could. Yet in 1975, he too had vowed never to return to Mount Ararat. As an idealistic twenty-five-year-old Christian ski bum from Wisconsin, he had dropped out of Biola College and taken his religious studies—and skis—to L'Abri, Switzerland, where he demonstrated an instant affinity for sheer cliffs and soaring summits. When he learned that his hero—Noah's ark scholar, author, and biblical apologist Dr. John Warwick Montgomery—had a visiting professorship up the road in Strasbourg, France, he wheeled across the border and presented himself at Montgomery's doorstep, insisting that he could help the professor conquer Ararat. A fast friendship formed, and Montgomery took his young protégé at his word, inviting Stuplich to drive a jeep from Switzerland to Turkey for the summer.

Stuplich spent the month working the fields below Ararat and generally getting acquainted with the local Kurds, while Montgomery sat back in Ankara waiting for permits. Stuplich made the most of his Turkish holiday by earning the local Kurds' trust and learning how to negotiate (and often bypass) the official permitting process.

"In those days," Stuplich recalled, "the Kurds laughed at the concept of getting Turkish permission to climb the mountain. The Kurds controlled the mountain, and I knew most of them by their first names. It put me in immediate demand as the leader of several expeditions."

All of that changed in 1975. As Stuplich remembered it, "The Turkish-Kurdish situation went bad."

In his years of scaling Ararat, Stuplich had weathered every frightful condition the mountain had to offer, including being taken for dead in a 1974 blizzard on the Parrot Glacier. Even that didn't prepare Stuplich for the nightmarish summer of 1975. Fearing arrest by Turkish authorities, he and a friend had leapt from a second-story hotel window and made a mad dash up Ararat's south face before fleeing the country.

"I was so scared," he said. "I told myself I would never go back to northeastern Turkey. Getting thrown in jail in Turkey is about as bad as standing before a firing squad."

Stuplich's resolve lasted for six years, and then his name unexpectedly showed up in one of Montgomery's books as "my intrepid advance scout."[1] This was a lofty endorsement from a leading ark scholar, and once again Stuplich was inundated with lucrative offers to head expeditions. He reconsidered his pledge and, in the end, couldn't resist the mountain's potent call. He still regards northeastern Turkey as one of the "scariest places on earth—the wild, wild west," an outlaw outback where one of the world's more disturbing undercurrents of social unrest poses a constant threat.

"Any time you have an ethnic group (the Kurds) occupying a land governed by another country (the Turks)," Stuplich said, "you have a political and military dynamic like that in Bosnia and the Balkans. At any time the situation can explode into sudden, unpredictable violence. The Kurdish concept of life can be described, quite literally, as 'give me liberty or give me death.' Our forefathers lived and breathed this concept, but over here you can *feel* it. The Kurds will eagerly die for their ethnic group and for the land they believe belongs to them. And in certain dicey situations atop Mount Ararat, you can find yourself in a position where they expect *you* to die for their ethnic group."

So far, we had all been fortunate as we toured hot spots around the globe, but sitting at dinner and listening to Stuplich spin his tales, I lamented that I would never see this land through his eyes. He knew Ararat and understood its people. For me, simply sitting in a café at the foot of Ararat—the site of some of my greatest disappointments—seemed cruelly ironic.

In the Anatolian dusk, watching the molten sun dissolve in the west, I felt a flicker of suspense. Confronted anew with the daunting challenge of Agri Dagi, I gave it one more glance, then whispered, "Tomorrow I will climb that painful mountain."

SPECIAL ARRANGEMENTS

We waited all day at a seedy youth hostel outside Dogubayazit to hear that the coast was clear. Word came at dusk, as our Kurdish guide and go-between, Micah, rushed in and told us to load our gear into his van.

"Quick! Quick!" he said, as we crowded into the back. We sat on our backpacks.

He drove us out of town, past a large convoy of Turkish troop transport trucks.

"See that?" Stuplich whispered. "Our payoff at work."

Well after sunset, Micah stopped to drop us off at the mountain's western edge. My watch said 9:30 PM. As we began to step out, a set of headlights appeared on the crest of a nearby hill.

"Close the doors! Close the doors!" Micah ordered.

We hunkered down again just as a Turkish military police car passed us going the other way. Micah sped off into the dark, making me wonder, *Why all the fear and secrecy? Hadn't someone been paid off?*

No one but Dick Bright and Micah knew the details of our "special arrangement," and Bright had told us not to ask questions. We had the distinct impression that some ranking Turkish officer charged with patrolling Mount Ararat had agreed to divert the troops long enough for us to get to the mountain. Judging by Micah's paranoia, we had an extremely narrow window.

Micah circled around to the previous drop-off point, but pitch-black darkness now made it impossible for us to see five feet beyond the van door. As we waited tensely for Micah's signal to go, our other young Kurdish guide saw another set of headlights coming and screamed, "Out, out, out!"

He leapt from the van, landing headfirst in a shallow ditch beside the road. Amazed by his fearless dive, I took a deep breath, glanced over at Stuplich, and jumped into the ditch alongside the Kurd. Seconds later, our entire team lay sprawled in the scrub-filled ditch, the oncoming truck's high beams shaving the tops of our heads.

As Micah sped off down the road and out of sight, I hated to see him go. He was an experienced climber who spoke good English, and he might have led us up the mountain. He chose instead to stay back and keep us posted on Turkish military movements via cell phone.

"I'll do you more good down here," he had reminded us as we jumped from the van like army paratroopers.

As both truck and van vanished in the distance, we picked ourselves up and began scrounging in the dark for our packs and supplies. Half of our gear had ended up on the opposite side of the road. Without flashlights, we gathered up what we could find and sprinted into the plain, trying to keep up with the young Kurd. Bright whispered that horses waited for us ahead, some 300 yards into the fearsome darkness.

A howling wind chilled me, and the soupy blackness struck dread to my heart. With only stars above, we had no shadows or visible contours to guide us across the knobby plain. I knew that dangerous predators—bears, wild dogs, and poisonous snakes— roamed the peak's marshy lowlands. I could deal with the dogs, but the prospect of stepping on a snake filled me with terror. With each step, I imagined crunching down on a nesting asp and feeling its fangs sink into my shin.

I plodded on, tripping down blind gullies and up invisible hillocks until we finally saw the dark silhouettes of five horses moving nervously in the distance. An elderly man (the young Kurd's father, I assumed) was struggling to keep them from spooking.

Thick tension filled the air. The horses, rearing and snorting against their bits, also felt it. For men who had supposedly garnered assurances of safety from ranking authorities, our guides seemed scared to death. They behaved as though the slightest noise would call down a Turkish battalion on our heads.

We lashed our packs to the horses and started off into the night.

"Wait!" Stuplich shouted. "I can't find my backpack!"

He ran from horse to horse, fumbling feverishly in the dark for his pack. The Kurds tugged the horses forward, but Stuplich jerked back. "I'm not going up that mountain without my backpack!" he snapped.

He knew—we all knew—the terrors of Mount Ararat, where summit temperatures can dip to extremely cold temperatures and the brutal winds are merciless. As he frisked the horses, I reached for my flashlight, cupping my hand over the bulb to diminish the beam. I had taken a step forward to help my friend when someone ripped the flashlight from my hand.

"No lights!" the elder Kurd hissed. "No lights." He fumbled with the switch until he had doused the bulb.

Stuplich found his pack strapped awkwardly to one of the horses and released a thankful sigh.

"We can go now," he said.

We resumed our manic march into the Anatolian steppe. I had never seen such a chaotic, panicky start to an expedition, and it made me uneasy.

"Why are the guides so petrified?" I asked Bright between breaths. "Weren't the Turks compensated for our safe passage?"

He shrugged and said, "We've just got to keep going."

I found no comfort in his words, but he was right. We had to keep going; there was no turning back. We trudged on through the darkness. Something was wrong, but I would worry in silence.

CHAPTER 11
THE KURDS

It isn't just the Turkish military that must grant permission to would-be Mount Ararat climbers. They have to gain passage from the Kurds as well. The Kurdish people believe that Ararat is their mountain, and that people walking on Ararat are walking on Kurdish territory. The Turkish government takes a different view.

The peak widely believed to harbor Noah's ark sits squarely within the ever-shifting borders of Kurdistan, the ill-defined Kurdish empire that at various times has occupied parts of Turkey, Iran, Iraq, and Syria. These fluid borders obscure the fact that Kurdistan is a real place with its own cities, language, culture, and beliefs. But to call Kurdistan a "country" stretches the definition.

Modernization, the erosion of traditional cultures, and at times, an unkind realignment of national borders have put immense pressure on the Kurdish people. The situation has forced them to fight for their lives and to identify themselves in opposition to hostile regimes in countries such as Iraq. Elsewhere, they do battle with established governments to regain control of their native lands. Like any displaced people, the Kurds desire a republic of their own, and to this end, Mount Ararat remains a coveted prize.

The Kurds living on the slopes of Mount Ararat have a deep hatred of the Turkish government, and a bitter civil war continues between them. The Kurds and the Turks have been at odds longer than anyone can remember. Until recently, Kurdish activity reduced the mountain to a hotly contested battle zone and kept the Turkish military on constant red alert. On a mountain so vast, it is impossible to contain the terrorists, and ark expeditions are especially vulnerable to attack.

A FAST HIKE

Our expedition team consisted of Bob Stuplich, Dick Bright, photographer David Banks, Canadian fireman George Kralik (invited along as our medic), the two skittish Kurds, and me. We hiked fast, blind to all but the plain's most obvious shapes and forms. I navigated by the muffled clop of horses' hooves. I had regained a degree of composure (having momentarily forgotten about the snakes) and for long, awestruck moments, I simply stared up at the mountain, now eerily silhouetted against the starry sky like an enormous, glowering pyramid. It looked so impossibly distant as to seem unapproachable.

Was it a mistake? Had we been dropped off at the right spot? Untold miles of hiking remained for us just to get to the mountain's base, before we could actually start climbing.

"It's going to take us forever to get there," I complained to Stuplich. "This can't be right."

"Shhhh!" the elder guide spit back through the pall.

Stuplich seemed amused by my naïveté and whispered, "What did you expect, Bob? This is the deal. If you want to climb Mount Ararat, it's a killer walk, start to finish."

"Shhhhh!" hissed the younger Kurd.

Suddenly I didn't feel much like climbing the mountain, but I kept walking. We trudged five miles across the plain, trekking through a meandering network of rugged ravines that girdled the lower basin before beginning a mild ascent. As we moved ever farther into the dense mantle of darkness, forging sharp, invisible draws and shuffling up rocky washes, each step took a toll on our already-tired legs and backs. For a few miles we stayed together, maintaining a compact perimeter around the horses, but as the hours passed, we each found our own stride, and the team gradually spread out across the slope. At times, I felt that I was climbing alone, marching silently in the dark. I would occasionally fall off pace and have to listen for the faint sound of hooves or boots kicking stones and trampling brush. All night, I stared at the mountain.

At about 1:30 AM, just as we began to enter the lower foothills, the moon came out, casting ivory light on the plain. This thin, glowing wafer seemed miraculous as it brightly lit the flats. To eyes dilated by numbing darkness, it ignited the heavens like a supernova.

We walked nonstop for eight weary hours up Ararat's western haunch, stopping to rest only when the first threads of dawn danced drowsily over the eastern plateau. By 5:30 AM, our furious pace had chopped a sizable chunk out of Ararat's plain. What had seemed an insurmountable gap a few hours earlier appeared in the cheerful morning light to be an achievable climb. Standing exhausted on a flattened patch of meadow at 9,000 feet, we pulled off our boots, unfurled our sleeping bags, and collapsed as if drugged for a much-needed short nap.

WILD DOGS AND GREEN SHALLOWS

I don't remember falling asleep, but I woke to see three Kangal sheepdogs circling us on the small knoll. I had heard of these mountain dogs. Jim Irwin once told me that they struck more fear in him than either the mountain or the military, and from the thin protection of my sleeping bag, I understood what he meant. The dogs circled and drooled, growling as if we looked like breakfast. They were square-jawed beasts, bred for battle and as stout and muscled as diesel trucks. Each wore a spiked collar and had jaws like a bear trap.

We played dead, tucking our heads inside our sleeping bags until we heard a faint voice calling from below the ridge. After a few moments, I peeked out to see a bedraggled Kurdish shepherd hiking up from the meadow. He whacked the dogs on the head with his staff, and they retreated, cowering in the grass like scolded pups.

Struggling to my feet with a stiff back, I thanked the shepherd for his timely entrance by offering him tuna and water from our packs. He devoured a tin of tuna in seconds. We also dug into our rations. After the marathon hike, our bodies craved protein, and the simple tuna tasted like prime tenderloin. I rolled mine up in flat bread like a burrito, devouring two cans in short order. I dreaded the brutal climb ahead, but the food and short nap had revived me.

Ararat loomed above us in craggy splendor as lavender clouds caressed its high mountain passes. The majestic, ice-capped peak filled the morning sky, bright blue glaciers glistening in the sun.

With our cranky horses resisting every move, we made a ponderous ascent up a tortured sequence of jagged slopes, cutting through loose rock and steep, scree-covered upgrades.

"Watch your ankles," Stuplich cautioned me. "The rocks up here are like bowling balls, always rolling out from under you."

For the next two hours, we rolled with them, hacking out a path to Lake Kop on Ararat's northern flank. I had seen the lake from the air and knew that the glacier-fed pool was the traditional low base camp of veteran ark searchers. It was a crucial first water refill stop, and we arrived just in time. We had consumed our water supplies, and we anticipated drinking our fill at Lake Kop.

The moment the horses caught the scent, they charged the lake and started sucking water like industrial Shop-Vacs. Arriving seconds later ready to follow suit, we stopped short. Instead of the crystalline mountain lake we had expected, we gazed at a slime pit pocked with hundreds of sheep hoofprints.

Kop's shallow waters, less than an acre in circumference, were as thick and green as pea soup, their filmy surface freckled with dollops of sheep dung. The sight and smell nauseated me, and though we felt dead on our feet and had only a few swigs left in our bottles, we turned away. There would be no refills at Lake Kop. Our guides spoke confidently of another stream bubbling out of the mountain at 11,000 feet, so we wrestled the engorged horses back to the path and resumed our climb into a curtain of clouds.

An hour later and 1,000 feet higher, we crested a hard-rock plateau to the joyous song of a glacial stream. I left my horse and walked toward it. The small rivulet was about ten inches wide, tucked behind a stand of boulders in a shallow gully. Shimmering in the sunlight, its milky gray waters flowed fifty feet down the slope then vanished into the volcanic turf. With our compact, reverse-osmosis filters, we pumped a few cups, repeating the process until the water filtered relatively clear and sweet. We sat on a rock, drinking until our heads hurt and our bellies were like cast-iron kettles.

Even in fire-baked Saudi Arabia, where it's impossible to quench one's thirst, water had never tasted so good. I could feel it replenishing my dehydrated body, inch by inch.

MUTINY ON THE MOUNTAIN

The horses were proving to be more of a hindrance than a help. They were slack-jawed and emaciated, their ribs sticking out like strings on a harp. Their spindly legs buckled under the weight of our packs, and one or more would often collapse to its knees. We had to tug on their reins to climb each serrated pass, and our progress was agonizingly slow. George Kralik's metal walking pole was bent and twisted from whacking his horse on the haunches to keep it moving.

"We should have left the horses behind," Stuplich complained. "It would have been easier climbing."

I agreed. We couldn't take the horses straight up the mountainside, but had to find paths they could travel. I lost track of all the box canyons we had to fight our way out of just to gain fifty feet of altitude. Less than a day in, the horses looked as if they might drop dead at any moment.

The Kurdish guides were only slightly less troublesome. Whenever the going got rough, they would go ballistic, throwing their hands in the air and jabbering that they couldn't go on. We had to get in their faces and demand that they keep going if they wanted to be paid.

At 7:30 PM, as the sun sank into the plain behind us, we reached 12,000 feet. A flat patch of wind-battered grass nestled in the shadow of a cold cliff wall. We had been charging hard for twenty-two straight hours, with only one short rest. We needed water again—our bottles were empty.

Too tired for words, we threw down a makeshift camp and unpacked our portable gas stove to heat a freeze-dried chicken casserole. As everyone else sprawled on the tundra too exhausted to move, I climbed the remaining fifty yards to a large slab of melting ice wedged in a stand of boulders. Below it, just as the Kurds had promised, sat a pool of melt-off, ten feet wide. I stared at it, stunned and disappointed. Like Lake Kop, the pool brimmed with sheep dung. This emergency water source had the same sickening smell and pea-green color we had rejected before.

If I drink this, I thought, *I'll have Montezuma's revenge until the year 2010.*

Yet as far as I could see, I had no other choice—I didn't expect to find a water fountain, and the guys below, cracked lipped, cotton mouthed, and dispirited, needed rehydration. We wouldn't make it very long without water, so against my strongest impulses I knelt down and stuck my filter into the turbid pool, siphoning out as many pollutants as possible before filling our plastic liter bottles. Returning to camp, I didn't have the heart to tell the others the condition of the water they so greedily guzzled. *Ignorance is bliss,* I thought. They didn't seem to mind the green-tinted water, and I tried not to think about it.

Over the next hour I cooked our dinner, serving the others but feeling too nauseated to eat. Either the water or the altitude had finished me for the day. The others nibbled a few bites and crawled into their tents. My own sleep was hard and fitful, fraught with strange, high-altitude dreams of cracking crevasses and thundering avalanches. In one, I drank from beautiful crystal mountain springs; in another, I battled angry nests of spitting snakes. I slept nonetheless, and that's what mattered. Tomorrow would be harder than today and far more dangerous. We had half a day to reach the lip of the Ahora Gorge, where Bright's ark supposedly lay.

Climbing Ararat goes beyond grueling; it is like being beaten by a blacksmith's hammer. After climbing it, I can confidently say that flying over the mountain in a helicopter is the preferred way to go. I had done that before, but there was no way that Bright and our group could have gotten a helicopter permit this time. The civil war on and around the mountain made it impossible. Our only hope of reaching Dick Bright's object was to slog up these slopes.

CHAPTER 12

TO THE SUMMIT!

I woke to the grating sound of Dick Bright and the Kurds bickering. At some time during the subzero night, our guides had unilaterally decided to retreat down the mountain with the horses. They had packed and were ready to go when Bright, half awake in his frost-glazed parka, began to boil. He threatened not to pay them for their services if they didn't continue the trek.

"No money!" he shouted. "Do you understand me? No money!"

After some boisterous arguing, the situation was resolved, but it cost us an early start. Stuplich and I crammed a couple of PowerBars and bottles of green-tinted water in our packs and marched out of the camp. Frustrated by the delay, we intended to scout a feasible route up to Parrot Glacier in advance of the team.

"We'll be right behind you," one of the team members shouted.

"Don't hold up the train," Stuplich snapped. "The days are short up here."

Still wrapped in morning mist and surly with whipping winds, the summit towered before us. The sun rose quickly, warming my stiff muscles as I climbed toward the humpback of Parrot Glacier and quietly pondered Ararat's stark solitudes and glacial heights.

PARROT GLACIER

Stuplich and I separated to find the best route up. Climbing up a steep, rugged field of cabin-sized boulders, I arrived at the stony ridge that runs east alongside Parrot Glacier. I waited in the glaring morning sun, taking in the vast, icy colossus in repose.

This leviathan block of ice got its name from Professor Friedrich Parrot, who in 1829 became the first foreigner in modern times to reach Ararat's stormy summit. In coming years, Parrot Glacier became a familiar haunt for ark searchers, who theorized that its prodigious ice cap made a logical grave for the ark.

Seeing the glacier up close had a strangely disorienting, hypnotic effect. Something about its glistening immensity seemed surreal and mystical. Set against the indigo sky—it seemed alive, a living, breathing organism that was yawning awake after a long hibernation. Every few minutes, it would emit a deep groan as if protesting our presence. A high-pitched creak would be followed by an elongated *craaack,* a clattering symphony of pings and pongs, and a booming thunderclap—a spectacular, earsplitting tantrum of shattered ice that triggered hideous echoes and sudden rockslides hundreds of yards below. My heart lodged in my throat as I watched the glacier snap and pop with such monstrous force.

I headed up the ridge. A short time later, Stuplich called out,

"Bob!" and I turned to see him coming toward me on the ridge, looking sweaty and concerned.

"I'm a little worried," he said, gazing intently back down the slope. "It's taking Bright and the others way too long to get up here. It'll be touch-and-go now whether we can make it up to the gorge and back down to camp before nightfall."

He inhaled huge gulps of thin mountain air while keeping an eye on the lower slope. He was quiet for a while, then pointed east toward a wide, icy moraine that frames the western rim of the Ahora Gorge.

"See that?" he said. "That's the boulder field where Jim nearly killed himself in '82. He only survived because he regained consciousness after the fall long enough to crawl inside his sleeping bag. He was a bloody mess when we found him, so we patched him up, put him on a donkey with Turkish commandos and rushed him down the mountain to a hospital." He shook his head. "He was hurt bad, but I'll never forget how upbeat he was, trying to make light of it. I couldn't believe it—he was trying to make *us* feel better."

Stuplich said he still cherished the memory of Irwin's showing up unannounced in Crested Butte a year later to ask forgiveness for getting angry and ignoring Bob's warning not to climb alone.

"He was a good man," Stuplich whispered. "A great man."

Up here on Parrot, nearly every boulder and crevasse triggered some memory for the veteran climber. He raised a hand to the east, pointing out the albino hump of Parrot, its back cracked and scarred by a lattice of sunken crevasses. In 1974, he had tried three times to find the hand-hewn beams that a Frenchman named Fernand Navarra claimed he had found in the bowels of a glacier high on the mountain in the 1950s. At the bottom of a gaping trench, Stuplich had located what appeared to be a huge, dark object—perhaps the remains of a large ship—but it sat submerged beneath one hundred feet of glacial water, well out of reach.

Bob Stuplich is nothing if not doggedly persistent. He climbed down the mountain, returned to Switzerland to get married, then immediately returned to Ararat with a wet suit, face mask, and snorkel. While his new bride waited out the first days of their honeymoon in Erzurum, Stuplich raced back up the mountain with his dive gear to probe the depths of the crevasse. But before he could dive, a blizzard blew in and stranded him for five days on the ice cap.

Word reached his wife that her new husband had perished in the brutal storm. A Turkish friend of Stuplich's told her to go home to America and that they would call her when the snows released his body in the spring. Fortunately, those reports failed to take into account his exceptional survival skills. He calmly weathered the storm and climbed down through deadly snowslides and avalanches, walking half dead into the hotel where his wife had already packed to leave.

"I don't think my wife fully appreciated our honeymoon," he deadpanned.

THE CEHENNEM DERE

Dick Bright and the others finally joined us on the ridge, without horses. Bob Stuplich waved them over.

"You took your sweet time," he said. "Now we've got to hurry, or we'll never make it back to camp in time."

We each took a sip from our bottles and grabbed our packs to leave, when from below the ridge we heard the menacing *womp, womp, womp* of helicopter rotors speeding over the rise.

"Get down! Get down!" Bright shouted.

Like panicked deer, we ditched our packs in the rocks and wedged ourselves under a granite overhang. I knew that if the Turkish military chopper—probably searching the peak for Kurdish rebels—saw us or mistook us for Kurdish freedom fighters, they would blast us off the mountain.

"Pray them away," Bright whispered desperately under his breath. "Pray them away."

For an hour and a half the chopper buzzed overhead, skimming Parrot Glacier to the fringe of the gorge, then all the way up to the summit. When the whirl of rotors finally faded below us and disappeared, we couldn't believe our good fortune.

We were safe for now, but we had suffered another devastating delay.

With daylight melting away, we pulled our packs out of the rocks and set off up a harrowing path through new vistas of sharp, rolling scree. For another two hours, we climbed into a darkening indigo sky. The younger Kurd said that he had never known such dry conditions up so high, and while the rare tempering of the weather gave us good climbing conditions, it forced us to drain our water reserves prematurely. My thirst was enormous.

At a glacial pool where Stuplich had dipped his cup on a prior trip, we found nothing but an alkaline dust hole. We were inching higher up the ridge toward a cluster of ice cliffs hanging from the North Canyon when Banks suddenly declared, "I hear water rushing."

We climbed another one hundred grueling yards up the crumbling slope to find a tiny puddle of glacier melt-off. Like our crazed horses at Lake Kop, I charged toward the water and knelt down to drink.

"Wait, Bob!" Stuplich shouted, yanking me back by my jacket cuff.

I spit out the water. "What?"

He pointed out the faint pinkish hue of the ice.

"See that color?" he asked. "That's bad bacteria. Drink that unfiltered and you'll be far sicker than you've ever been."

I tore open my pack and pulled out my filter. After pumping some water, we drank deeply, took a few deep breaths, and began struggling up the last stretch of icy ground to the overhanging Cehennem Dere. I had seen it in dozens of pictures, but nothing had prepared me for the visual impact of this colossal cleft of ice rising into the skyline. It seemed precariously perched on the crater-edge of eternity—an arctic platform to the heavens. From its enormous floor, we caught our first stunning glimpse of the Ahora Gorge.

Strapping on our crampons, we treaded carefully across the huge, sloping dome of ice, carefully lifting and planting one foot in front of the other on the slick, ice-glazed surface.

"It's like climbing across an ice-covered basketball," I carped to Bright, aware that the tiniest slip would send me sliding feet first into the gorge's hungry maw.

For a few hundred yards, we let Bright lead us single-file across the ice, tethered by a cord for safety. But as the hour grew later and our progress remained ploddingly slow, Bob Stuplich made an executive decision: He untied the rope and told us to set off on our own.

"What if someone falls?" I asked.

Without a trace of sarcasm, he said, "Don't fall."

Step by step, we traversed the Cehennem Dere, padding alongside creaking crevasses, over fragile ice bridges, and into bowled-out ice pockets. In a windblown snowdrift, we came upon the mummified remains of some unrecognizable one-horned beast, its carcass protruding from the melting ice. From its long, serpentine horn, we surmised that it was an ibex, a rugged, wild mountain goat uniquely adapted to these heights. I shuddered, thinking, *If Ararat proved too much for that poor beast, what chance do I have?*

Our legs were cramped from oxygen deficit. Arctic glare burned our faces and blistered our skin. Dazed with exhaustion, I carelessly clicked my crampons together, releasing the spring lock on my right ice boot. Before I realized what had happened, I found myself staring over the edge of the soaring cliff, standing one-legged on the ice dome with my crampon dangling by a strap. I couldn't sit or plant my foot, and I didn't dare move. One touch of a boot rubber on ice would send me hurtling into the gorge at the exact spot where Stuplich had warned us that many had slipped off the mountain.

Breathing hard and trying not to panic, I began to teeter, losing my balance. Just then, Stuplich appeared from nowhere and lent me his shoulder. Balancing myself against his body, I slowly reached down and reattached my crampon.

"Thanks, Bob," I said. He just nodded and kept walking.

THE GORGE

Our team spread out across the Cehennem Dere at intervals of fifty to one hundred yards, treading lightly over fragile ice bridges and crevasses made nearly invisible by the swirling clouds and dense shadows. At this almost 16,000-foot altitude, our eyes played tricks on us because of oxygen deficiency, blurring the edges of the fatal gorge.

Suddenly, Dick Bright called out, "This is the place! That's where I saw the ark."

He pointed into the breathtaking canyon. We followed his direction along the ice, peering over the edge into a chasm that was a mile deep and over a mile wide. Its jagged contours and depths seemed distorted and out of scale, and I found it hard to focus. Its sheer magnitude overwhelmed me. I wobbled a little, and Stuplich placed a steadying hand on my shoulder.

"Don't sweat it," he said. "Most men's knees turn to mush at their first sight of the gorge."

We stood there for a long while, trying to scan the flinty cliffs and shadows. At last, Bright spotted his target—a large, angular object embedded in the opposite cliff face. It had a sharp nautical nose and angled down from the side of the gorge. We surveyed it from several angles with our binoculars, and as I feared, it was nothing but ice-covered rock sticking out of the canyon wall.

I climbed all the way up here for this?

Perhaps it was because I was at the end of an exhausting journey, but the sight struck me as depressingly anticlimactic. I wanted to get off the peak as quickly as possible. Instead, we stayed on the rim as long as we could, peering at the gorge from every angle. We scoured the cliffs, probed its trenches, and videotaped the canyon from top to bottom, but saw no ark, no boat, no object warranting further time and attention. Though I had doubted Dick's claims from the start, my heart sank as I realized that I had been right. I would have been overjoyed to have been wrong. So much pain and effort for nothing!

My disappointment couldn't compare to Bright's. He stood glassy-eyed and crestfallen on the rim of the abyss, having climbed this heartbreaking slope three times in the past two months. He didn't want to go down, but to stay a minute longer would be our undoing. As the sun banked slowly below the summit, the temperature began to plummet.

As it was, we had stayed an hour too long. We would never make it down now before dark. Thirsty, hungry, and exhausted as we were, the threat of mental lapses now loomed large. Oxygen deprivation could slow our progress or send someone absently walking off a cliff.

With time running out, we gathered our resolve and began to retrace our steps across the Cehennem Dere, knowing that to stray a step or two outside of our tracks could kick out a hidden crevasse.

My watch said 4:00 PM. Dense clouds and cold settled in around us. It would be dark by 7:30 PM, but we still had a four-hour descent to high camp. The math didn't look good, and thanks to the Turkish army, we couldn't use headlamps or flashlights. I imagined our bedraggled crew climbing down this tortuous route in the dark.

"Let's go, men!" I shouted. "We're in a race against darkness!"

Cruising down the ice cap while shooting video of the sunset, David Banks and I found ourselves in front of the others. On the loose sand ridge below the Cehennem Dere, I realized that Bob Stuplich, George Kralik, and our guide had lagged behind. Further back, Dick Bright shuffled morosely across the ice. He was struggling. Exhausted from the climb and demoralized by his failure at the Ahora Gorge, he had lost his edge. We waited for the others to catch up.

"I could have sworn it was the ark," he kept muttering as we turned back toward base camp.

I had seen it all before. The gorge's shadowy depths, uncommon lighting, and basaltic geology could trick the most sincere observer into believing that he had seen the ark. Bright couldn't have looked more dejected. Shortly into our descent, his crampon speared the ice and flipped him head-over-heels down the glacier toward a huge crevasse. He somehow caught a crease with his ice ax at the last possible second and dragged himself to a stop, his legs flailing over the edge. Kralik raced back up the slope and pulled him out—a fatality narrowly averted.

Now we were in trouble. Any hope of making it back to camp as a group before dark was long gone. Then, as I picked my way down the boulder field, I heard Stuplich screaming from above.

"Bob, we're hung up here. Bright's boot is falling apart."

It hardly surprised me. His leather alpine boots, well past their prime, had served him nobly through the years, but this trip had pushed them too far. The rubber sole of his right boot had split away and flapped against the rocks.

What else could go wrong? I wondered. We had spent thousands of dollars on travel and equipment, and now the expedition's outcome hinged on a piece of bad footwear. Stuplich shouted that they would duct tape Bright's boot together and hope it lasted. He would be coming down one of the steepest stretches of one of the most dangerous mountains in the world—in total darkness. It didn't sound like much of a plan.

"Are you guys going to be okay?" I shouted back.

"Go on ahead!" Stuplich yelled. "We'll get Dick down somehow."

For three days, this potential disaster had been building; now the consequences of every delay, every argument, every horse spitting out its bit stared us square in the face. Even in broad daylight Bright's predicament would have been a costly momentum killer. With darkness closing in, people might die on the mountain this night. There were too many blind turns and forked ravines between us and high camp for us to find our way back quickly in the dark.

I didn't have the strength to climb back up, and I knew that I was of no use to the others where I was. Surveying the terrain below, I realized that our only hope would be for me to make a mad dash down to camp before the last flicker of sunset disappeared, then find some way to guide the others in. Maybe from below I could do something to help.

I turned to Banks. "Can you make it on your own?"

"Yeah," he said, clearly too spent to keep up. "Go on. I'll wait for the others."

I knew they would catch up with him soon enough, so I headed down the mountain, moving as fast as I could without killing myself, and stutter-stepping into the North Canyon to the narrow ridge beside Parrot Glacier. From above, the glacier looked like a white serpent coiling into the valley, but my burning legs and lungs kept me from enjoying the splendid scenery. I knew I couldn't stop for even a moment's rest.

During extreme circumstances in the past—in countless desperate moments in remote locales when I felt like giving up—I learned simply to grit my teeth, block out the pain, and keep pushing. I knew that even entertaining the notion of rest might mean the difference between surviving or not. So I settled into a mechanical rhythm, mindlessly moving my feet, scooting from rock to rock, and letting the bowling effect roll me along.

As I scrambled through the boulder field, it occurred to me that prior to the 1800s, the Armenians thought it was physically impossible for a human to reach the top of Mount Ararat. Two centuries later, God willing, we would be up—and off—in three days. I now understood why they called it the "painful mountain."

As night descended, I staggered, half delirious, into base camp. The elder Kurd sat off by himself, casually smoking a cigarette. He watched me in silence. Within minutes, the entire slope would vanish under a black veil that would obliterate all shadows and structures that might help the others feel their way down. I calculated that they would have reached the steepest part of the slope by now, perhaps perishing in the treacherous boulder field.

Without a minute to waste, I groped about in the dark to find my tent, crawled inside, and ripped open my pack, rifling frantically through clothes and camping gear in search of a small, plastic medallion—a fluorescent green light patch with an adhesive backing. When I broke the seal, the tiny camping light combined its chemicals and emitted a soft, green glow.

Stuplich had laughed when he saw me stash it in my pack in Erzurum. "That's a waste," he said. "You'll never use it."

Now it looked like our only hope—a light too faint to be seen by Turkish patrols below but, I hoped, bright enough to guide the climbers down. I crawled outside and stuck it to the outside wall of the tent that faced uphill toward the climbers, then sat down and prayed that they would see it.

I waited, exhausted by my high-speed workout. I knew I should eat, but I felt sick. I sat there in dead silence for two hours, watching, waiting, and listening. At about 9:00 PM, I heard footsteps dragging heavily through the rubble. Slowly they appeared, one by one, like zombies from the night—Banks, Kralik, Bright, and the young Kurd—staggering into camp looking shell-shocked and dead on their feet. As they passed, each mumbled a grateful, barely audible thanks. Then they either crawled into their tents or simply collapsed on their sleeping bags in the open air. As expected, Stuplich brought up the rear, shuffling into camp like a weary shepherd trailing his flock. He walked over to me.

"Bob," he said, "that's the best thing you could've done. I'm glad you brought that little light."

"No problem," I said as we joined the others, now snoring in their sleeping bags. No one moved until mid-morning the following day.

CHAPTER 13
RUNNING FOR OUR LIVES

Again I woke to the agitated, shrilly bickering Kurds. Fearing that Bright was at it again over horses or money, I rolled out of my sleeping bag and saw him sitting alone on a rock, looking gloomy. The Kurds were huddled off by themselves near the horses, shouting into the cell phone.

"They're talking with Micah," Bright said. "He called to warn us that Turkish soldiers are on the mountain." I looked at the Kurds. They were fussing and fuming, looking more disturbed than ever.

"They're scared to death," Bright continued. "Micah, too. He says he's very afraid for us." He stared into the distance, then added, "Micah says he won't be able to pick us up where he dropped us off. We'll have to go down a different way."

That got my attention.

"A different way? What do you mean, Dick, a different way?"

"Remember the helicopter? There was a gun battle yesterday near Lake Kop; it stirred up the Turkish military, and now they're combing the mountain for rebels. Eleven people were killed—seven Turks and four Kurds. They'll have the north slope strapped down tighter than a drum. We'll have to descend down the cliffs on the southwest side of the mountain."

The southwest cliffs? I had never heard of anyone descending there, and I doubted that even Stuplich knew the terrain, but we had no time to debate the point. The terrified Kurds had already packed the horses and began shouting at us, "We go! We go!"

I started to roll up my tent, but suddenly remembered something.

"Wait!" I shouted. "We need to filter some water."

We raced back up the hill and found the fetid puddle where I had filtered water two days earlier; but when the others saw it, they insisted that we not only filter but boil it. It seemed to take forever for our two little camp stoves to boil the water in our tiny cook pots, and even then it looked undrinkable. Kralik and Banks poured instant coffee crystals in their bottles to try to mask the rancid taste and scummy appearance, but they might as well have dabbed perfume on a warthog. In the end, we had neither the time nor the firepower to stock up on water. The Kurds were on the verge of a nervous breakdown and threatened to abandon us if we didn't get moving.

DRY TIMES WITH THE KURDISH UNDERGROUND

It disturbed me to see the raw fear on the Kurds' faces. They kept rubbing their foreheads, wringing their hands, and shifting their weight from foot to foot. "We go! We go!"

I took their edginess with a grain of salt. They had been acting like this the whole trip, but I knew our predicament had deteriorated when Bright repeated, "Micah is scared for us."

We set off down the mountain at a silent, steady clip, keeping our eyes on the slope directly in front of us. It was soon clear that we would run out of water long before we reached bottom. No one knew when or if we would pass any streams or glacial pools, and on Ararat's porous, bone-dry slope, the chances of stumbling upon potable water were doubtful. We carefully monitored our intake, taking sips only when we couldn't stand it anymore, and kept our ears cocked to hear the distant trickle of water.

The sun bore down as we descended the small bowl of Lake Kop shortly after noon. Sweating from exertion and chafing under my load, I fantasized that its waters might somehow have cleansed themselves. Surely we had been mistaken when we were here last; its foul appearance had been a cruel trick of the sun played on weary brains. Walking to the bank erased those illusions—Kop's waters stank more than ever. The horses didn't care, and I envied them as they filled their bellies. We still had a few cloudy swigs left in our bottles, so no one thought to filter a bottle or two for good measure before we left—a decision we would later regret.

From Lake Kop, we traced a jagged route to the southwest side of the mountain, traversing high meadows and the bristly ridges of the upper foothills. The way down was just as laborious as the trek up—we pulled the horses down the steep grade, pulled them up knifelike ridges and down ravines filled with loose rubble, proceeding foot by foot, hour by hour, mile by mile into vast, unfamiliar tracts.

Every hour or so, we crossed paths with a changing cast of

Kurdish sheepherders who mysteriously appeared from behind a bluff or over a rise to send us off in a new direction. "Go down that way," they said, pointing with their staffs. Or, "Duck into this canyon and down that pass," and we would shift course accordingly. I didn't immediately realize it, but these silent messengers comprised Ararat's famous Kurdish underground—a stealth guerilla corps of sheepherders, villagers, and ethnic terrorists, invisible to outsiders but strategically situated for mountain warfare.

It seemed similar to the European resistance movement of World War II, when local farmers assisted freedom fighters to sabotage the German army's advance. Up here, everyone looked out for everyone else. These silent warriors led us from one camp to the next, sharing intelligence on the Turkish maneuvers below. They always knew precisely where the Turkish military patrolled the foothills, and we passed three, then four Kurdish camps spread across the mountain. Together, they kept us out of harm's way.

OVER THE CLIFF

Afternoon dissolved into dusk, steep canyons spilled into high foothills, and mild breezes gave way to sweltering heat as we entered a lower patchwork of smooth, wide pastures that bled into long, lazy valleys. Although we were desperately thirsty and tired, this gently rolling southwestern route was a pleasant surprise. It seemed easier than the way up. *Why would the Turks ignore this gradual decline?* I wondered.

As we arrived at a flat, grassy plateau where another large herd of sheep grazed, a shepherd told us to hunker down in the tall grass and wait for sundown. The pasture was exposed in broad daylight, and the adjacent slope, he said, had been crawling with Turkish troops all day. We waited for two hours, until the last rays of sun melded into a crimson sunset. At dusk, we walked the horses over to a wide ledge.

Dick Bright peered over the edge into the tumbling moraine. "We've got to climb down there to reach the plain," he said.

I suddenly understood why the Turks never patrolled these cliffs. No fool would ascend this suicide precipice. With a moonless night now upon us, we shimmied down the ledge, slipping and clawing down the sheer granite cliff wall into a waking nightmare. The near-vertical pitch would have made for treacherous climbing during daylight, but at night, with horses, our prospects were dismal.

I have terrible night vision, and without a trail I had to fumble my way down every foot of that slope, using my ski pole to probe the empty black spaces in front of me. Pulling the horse along, I would take a hesitant step down into the rolling scree, probe the dark, take another small step, and then another, sometimes poking my pole where the next step should be and feeling nothing. One misstep could send me plunging off the cliff.

The horses could see in the dark; they whimpered and whined, making pitiful crying sounds as they wobbled and heaved under their heavy loads. Skidding and clopping down the winding course, their hooves kicked up sparks on the granite. I followed the sparks of the horse in front of me. Keeping a hand on its bony haunches, I tapped my pole for a foothold, then nudged the horse along and felt my way down through the crumbling rubble.

If the Kurds knew a better way down, they didn't share it with us. I could hear them chattering frantically back and forth. They were as uneasy as I was, cursing the horses and refusing to wait on any of us. In the interminable darkness, our team soon spread itself across the cliff face. It was every man for himself.

"This is mountain goat country, not horse country," I complained. Stuplich was slipping along behind me, prodding his horse down the terraced granite. At one point, a horseshoe scraped violently across the granite behind me. As I turned, Stuplich's horse rammed into me, knocking my breath out and sending me flying fifteen feet off the ledge into a ravine. Miraculously, I landed on my back in soft sand.

Dusting myself off and thanking God that I hadn't hit my head on a rock, I wondered if we were going to make it. I didn't like my answer: *The odds aren't in our favor. I'm parched dry with thirst and sweating so hard my kidneys ache; we have no water; my next step could send me over a cliff, and we've still got hours to go in pitch blackness.* I scolded myself. *Why didn't we filter more water at Lake Kop? It didn't look so bad. . . .*

No matter how hard I prayed, I couldn't escape the awful fact that we still had a long way to go. We had to get these horses down the cliff, and we had to do it without lights.

Hour by agonizing hour, we made our way down into the valley, where we encountered yet another sea of rocks. I kept praying for the moon to rise as it had on our first night out, but the sky remained so dark that I couldn't see Dick Bright walking five feet ahead of me.

We caught up with the Kurds in the valley and found them chattering with Micah on the cell phone. In yet another shocking bit of bad news, Micah said that the military had formed a noose around the base of the mountain, and he couldn't pick us up where we had originally planned. It meant walking another five miles across the plain to meet him at an alternate site. My heart sank, but I didn't have time to feel sorry for myself. In that instant, military flares exploded over our heads, shattering the dark with garish hues of pink. Dogs started barking, and we could hear trucks grinding their gears in the distance. The panicked Kurds set off in a wild sprint across the valley floor, dragging the horses and screaming, "Go! Go! Go!"

THE RACE TO THE ROADWAY

We stumbled through shallow gullies and over sharp-edged rocks that littered the valley floor. My back hurt, my legs were on fire, and my heart tumbled in my chest. My natural optimism was quickly evaporating in the heat of fear, and my stomach clenched in the cold darkness. I wondered if we were going to make it.

We pressed on, barely staying ahead of the pale overhead glow of the flares shot skyward by the advancing soldiers. I could see them scouring the rocky terrain with their flashlight beams. Our Kurdish guides stayed in front of us, obviously as frightened as we were. They jerked at the reins of the spindly packhorses that wobbled under the heavy climbing gear we had hurriedly lashed to their backs. Fatigue from four days of relentless scaling up and down this enormous mountain had taken its toll on our five-member climbing team. We staggered through the night on the edge of collapse, sucked dry by dehydration and exertion.

As we continued across the rocky field to where we hoped our van and driver were waiting, another flare popped overhead. This time it was close—too close. We dove to the dusty ground, scrambling for cover in the sparse, scrubby brush. It was a wasted effort. We might be able to lie low, but our horses couldn't. Our pursuers would probably see them and know that we couldn't be far away. Nonetheless, we lay still until the flare burned out.

The moment it died, the Kurds jumped up and frantically yanked at the horses' bits, all but dragging them into a dry streambed that offered us some protection. We found it easier to walk on the sand, and soon we were able to put some distance between ourselves and the soldiers. At times, I was certain that I couldn't take a single step more—my pulse pounded in my temples, my tongue was leather, and my legs were bags of cement—but adrenaline and the fear of capture propelled me.

The van and driver were supposed to be a short distance ahead, but when we reached the designated pickup point, no one was there.

"We go! We go!" the Kurds insisted, yanking the horses forward. I could hear the terror in their voices.

Dave Banks, our cameraman, dropped to his knees, gulping for air. "Can't we rest here just a minute?" he asked.

No one answered. No one needed to. The sound of the dogs became louder, and the flashlight beams drew closer. At any second, I expected a helicopter to zoom across the steppe and swoop down on us. Whatever "special arrangements" had been made with the military had clearly broken down. Banks forced himself to rise and we pressed on.

SAFE AT LAST

Around 2:00 AM, we finally crested a small knoll and saw the flashing headlights of Micah's van. It was a beautiful sight. The Kurds circled the horses to make sure that no one had followed us, and as we approached the van, the doors burst open and five Kurds jumped out to grab our mounts. Without a word, our guides vanished with them into the night.

We hopped into the van and Micah sped down the road. No one spoke until we were safely out of range of the flares. Finally, Micah turned and gave us a broad grin. "Welcome home, gentlemen."

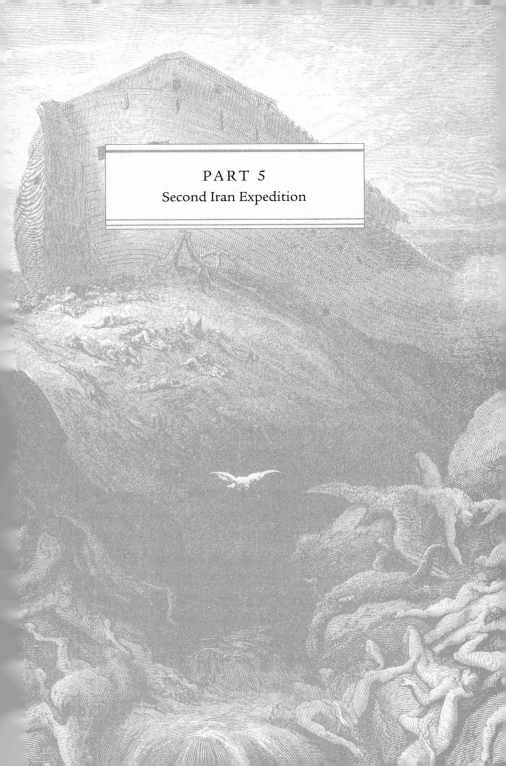

PART 5
Second Iran Expedition

CHAPTER 14

MOUNT SABALON

Northwest Iran, September 8, 1999

With the painful mountain behind me, I vowed once again never to return to Ararat. The next day, Bob Stuplich and I left Dick Bright and the others in Erzurum and caught a late-night flight to Iran, via Istanbul. When we landed in smoky, teeming Tehran, slightly the worse for wear, the airport was abuzz with activity, even though it was 3:00 AM. Passing through the terminal, we met our new guide as he waved a placard bearing my predictably misspelled name: *Mr. Bob Kornuk.* Ali (not the driver from my first trip) was short of stature, soft-eyed, and gentle. He seemed a little nervous, but competent and eager to please. A professor of education at Tehran University, Ali was able to interpret the country through the eyes and mind of a scholar. On my last trip, I had appreciated

Fatima's assistance, but in light of Iran's strict gender class system, it seemed far better for me to be traveling with a man. Ali came highly recommended, with solid standing among the Iranian tourism people who had helped us secure our visas.

We took a cab to a hotel in the center of town, and all I wanted to do was collapse into bed. Every inch of my body ached from the rigors of Mount Ararat. But before I could even take off my shoes, a loud knock sounded at the door. Outside stood my old friend Larry Williams; our new cameraman, Brad Houston; and a man I'll call Phil Trahern to protect his privacy. The three men had arrived in town two days earlier and had busied themselves setting our itinerary and doing some preliminary research.

We planned to drive directly from Tehran to Kermanshah to kick off my two-year plan to canvass northwest Iran. We would systematically work our way up the Zagros Mountains, interviewing as many Iranians as possible on legends and theories of the ark, and then head east across the interior. Because I had searched the southern Zagros on my last trip, this expedition would begin at Kermanshah, in the central Zagros, and cut north toward the Iranian province of Azerbaijan.

Although it was late and I needed sleep, Williams and Trahern said that they had news.

"What's got you so excited?" I asked.

They answered in unison: "We found *Caz-been!*"

I invited them into my room—this story I had to hear. I knew of "Cazbeen" from the Ed Davis interviews, because he had mentioned it often. He and Badi had driven through Cazbeen—or somewhere that sounded like it—en route to the mountain of the ark. This meant that Cazbeen was a critical landmark, but we had never been able to locate a place by that name. I had always sus-pected that if we could solve that enigma, it might give us a better starting point.

Davis and Badi had traveled without a map, and Davis couldn't remember where Cazbeen was or how it was spelled. It set us to guessing, and for a long time I thought Davis might have meant "Cas-peen," as in the Caspian Sea, but nothing clicked.

"So how did you guys find this place?"

Larry pointed to our guide and said, "We just asked Ali about possible sites for the town, and he immediately said, 'Oh, you must mean Qazvin. It is just north of Hamadan, west of Tehran.'" When Ali pointed it out on the map, Larry saw that it lay on the main route to 16,000-foot Mount Sabalon. "We just stood there, staring dumbly at the map. It seemed too easy. We had never considered that in Farsi, the *b* sound is spelled with a *v*. But it made perfect sense. *Cazbeen* was really *Qazvin*."

I stared at Williams, not thinking too clearly in my foggy state.

"Don't you realize what this means, Bob?" Williams said. "This is great news. Phil and I drove up there yesterday. From what we could see, it fits Davis's account."

On the map, Sabalon sat 250 miles north of Hamadan. Ed Davis had said that he could see the mountain range from the city where he and Badi had begun their journey. When I was in Hamadan, it was so smoggy that I couldn't see a mile, let alone a distant moun-tain. On the maps, Sabalon is the tallest mountain in the northern direction, and it sat within the prescribed driving distance of Hamadan, though it was somewhat of a stretch. I wondered if Da-vis could really see the mountain peaks from so far away. Perhaps he was describing the advancing foothills that lead to this massive mountain range. Regardless, these were compelling new leads that put us hot on Ed Davis's trail in Iran.

This raised a problem, however. In Iran, you go only where you have permission to go, and our visas only allowed us to travel south to Kermanshah, well out of range of Sabalon and clearly in the wrong direction. With Larry Williams and Phil Trahern standing next to my bed waiting for my response, I made a spot decision. "We're scrapping everything and heading to Sabalon. We've got to see this mountain."

In Iran, it's never a good idea to change plans abruptly. For Americans, it's a bit like hanging a pork chop around your neck and strolling through a kennel—you're bound to attract unwanted attention. Simply to enter the country, foreigners must obtain visas, secure a government-appointed guide, and then file a detailed schedule of activities with the authorities. Straying off course could only invite calamity. Given America's strained history with Iran, any U.S. citizen fortunate enough to procure a visa—even under today's supposedly "relaxed" tourism policies—is closely monitored. Iranian authorities still deeply mistrust all Americans.

When I informed Ali of our change of plans, his jaw dropped. When he saw that I meant business, he slapped his forehead and moaned.

I felt bad. We had created a touchy situation, and I understood his dilemma. Ali had superiors to report to—the secret police, for instance—who would hold him accountable for any irregularities. But I didn't have the luxury of wasting an entire trip touring the central Zagros when this new data clearly pointed us north toward Mount Sabalon. I apologized profusely.

"I'm sorry, Ali, but we are going to Sabalon. We leave in the morning."

LAND OF DIVERSITY

Early the next morning, Larry Williams, Bob Stuplich, Phil Trahern, Brad Houston, Ali, and I jammed our packs and equipment into a ten-seat charter van and headed northwest toward Ardabil, located in the hot plains around Mount Sabalon.

Traveling 250 miles in Iran is not like traveling 250 miles in the United States. Iran's main roads, though mostly passable, feature a driving culture that requires plenty of stopping and loitering along the roadside to chat with the locals about the weather and such. In our case, this provided our driver ample time to check frequently under the hood, pour water into the radiator, and buy a soda.

It quickly became apparent that over-the-road travel in Iran is a hot, grinding ordeal. The rambling byways convinced me that Davis and Badi could never have reached Mount Ararat in Turkey in eight to ten hours. Traveling from Hamadan to reach Ararat in a WWII military truck at a top speed of 35 mph on the rutted Iranian roads would have taken them four or five days.

The road took us into Qazvin, a dusty, nondescript town of shadowy shops and well-kept mosques not far from Hamadan. We drove through monotonous desert foothills and dry, stubble-filled prairies, passing rugged wheat fields and sod-busted farm plots worked by men in long sleeves and women in flowing scarves and ankle-length dresses. Ten hours later, near the southwestern edge of the Caspian Sea—less than sixty miles from Mount Sabalon—the landscape abruptly changed. From harsh, withering desert heat, we transitioned into a green land of palms and ferns.

We stopped for the night in the town of Rasht, a pleasant village on the southwest coast. From Rasht, it was just a short drive to hot and dry Ardabil, nestled in the heart of Iranian Azerbaijan, eighty miles south of the border of the former Soviet Azerbaijan.

When we arrived at our hotel, Ali began pleading with us to abandon our forbidden course. He wrung his hands, slapped his forehead, and implored Allah to intercede. Ali had grown increasingly panicked at the prospect of the secret police tracking our journey. It made me nervous too. I knew he had his orders and wanted to do everything by the book, but circumstances being as they were, I decided to throw the book out the window. My brief time in Iran had taught me that it is better to ask forgiveness than permission. I knew that if we asked consent for every change, we would never get anywhere. If we couldn't complete the survey in our limited time, we would go home empty-handed.

"Ali," I insisted, looking him square in the eye, "we *must* continue."

SABALON SPLENDOR

The next day, as we drove along the north side of the mountain toward Ghotor Suee—hot sulfur springs that Ali had told us about—I noticed vineyards. I turned to Larry and he nodded, remembering that Davis had spoken of seeing an ancient-looking vineyard at a remote village near the mountain's base, some plots so old that their vines were as thick and gnarled as twisted oaks. This never fit the profile of Mount Ararat, whose surrounding plain has no significant agriculture. The only problem with these Iranian vineyards was that they were of normal size. Ed Davis was very explicit about how big the trunks had been in the vineyards he saw.

Genesis 9:20 says that Noah planted a vineyard soon after leaving the ark. The presence of vineyards around Mount Sabalon squares with the region's status as the cradle of modern civilization. Traces of the oldest known wine, dating from about 5000 BC, surfaced recently in northwest Iran. Archaeologists who excavated the ruins of Hajji Firuz Tepe, just below Lake Urmia, scraped the residue of wine from inside an ancient clay jar. This wine predated the next oldest known wine by some two thousand years.

Seeing the gently sloping hills and quaint farming villages, noble orchards, and majestic vineyards, I wondered, *Could these glistening fields of grapes, draped across the valley like a jade necklace, have descended from Noah's seedlings?*

SULFUR CITY

Our driver pulled off the main road and steered up a narrow dirt path into Sabalon's steep foothills. As we climbed, quiet glens of rolling orchards and vineyards turned into small mountains overlooking deep canyons. To the warring ancients, these immense, rugged mountains formed an impenetrable fortress that I found visually spellbinding.

At a confluence of steep canyons riding up the shin of Sabalon's spiny foothills, we came upon a small town that we dubbed "Sulfur City" because of its overpowering rotten-egg smell. The town's real name is Ghotor Suee, a Farsi term meaning "water that cures the wound." In ancient times, Ali explained, nomads brought their enfeebled camels to these therapeutic springs for healing.

Ghotor Suee was a lively, primitive-looking town that could have been an adobe and mud set from *Raiders of the Lost Ark*. On the afternoon we arrived, its wood-plank storefronts were bustling with visitors from across Iranian Azerbaijan. Nomads, mountain folk, farmers, and shepherds had come to revel in the town's lively ambiance and soak in the famous hot springs.

The government recently raised a crude, concrete privacy wall around the springs, allowing men and women to take turns soaking in the sandy-bottomed pool's tepid brown waters. At the river's edge, a shepherd slaughtered a sheep, idly tossing the fat, blood, and entrails into the stream. Soon a hungry crowd feasted on flame-seared kebabs and nibbled on the poor beast's organs, now twisted and sizzling on a stick. No matter where we went, the pungent smell of rotten eggs prevailed.

"Do you think these were the springs Davis spoke of?" Brad Houston asked.

"Well," I shrugged, "the smell fits. Davis told me he smelled a rotten-egg odor as he went up the mountain."

We parked the van next to the stream and began canvassing the village. With Ali's help, I sought an audience with the village elders, and after several minutes of animated dialogue with a group of men sitting on a stone-cobbled porch, Ali ushered me up a flight of stairs to the second-floor of a bungalow overlooking the creek. Larry Williams and Brad Houston followed me upstairs, and we all sat down on the mat-covered floor of the bungalow, leaving Phil Trahern and Bob Stuplich outside to mingle with the crowds.

Tea was served, and Ali explained our mission to the village patriarch, a gray-haired, sunken-eyed man of about eighty. Despite the hot weather, the old man wore a heavy, Persian-print wool sweater. When the formalities ended, Ali translated as I asked the old man a series of questions. A gaggle of onlookers gathered in the doorway to listen.

"Have you, or any of the other men in this village, seen or heard of Noah's ark on Mount Sabalon?"

Ali translated my question and the old man's response.

"He says that his grandfather and great-grandfather knew where it was."

"Where what was?" I asked.

"Noah's ark."

"Did they see it?"

"Yes," Ali translated. "He says they have seen it."

With that, the old patriarch began to fidget, and the room now rippled with tension. Williams folded his arms, trying to look nonchalant. Then I asked, "Does he, the elder, know where it is?"

Ali slowly repeated my question. The old man sat stone-faced for nearly a minute, then gave a slight nod.

"Yes," Ali said, somber faced. "He knows . . . but . . ."

"But what?" I was impatient.

"The elder says he knows about the ark . . . but . . ." He paused to ask the elder something, then continued. "He wants us to know that he still believes in the Koran."

I was confused. "I don't understand."

"The author of the Koran," Ali explained, "was Islam's founder, Muhammad. The Koran has its own story of the Flood and of Noah and the boat." He paused, nodding politely toward the patriarch. "But its tradition does not include Mount Sabalon. The ark came to rest on a mountain called Jabal Judi."

I knew about Jabal Judi. Koran scholars place it vaguely in any number of locations from Syria to Saudi Arabia. At one time or another throughout the Near East, perhaps a dozen peaks have been named Jabal Judi. But for this elderly gentleman, the point had grave implications. Even to hint that the ark rested on Mount Sabalon rather than Jabal Judi was at best to call Muhammad mistaken and at worst, a liar. It could get the patriarch thrown in jail for religious heresy, or worse. Anyone caught suggesting that the holy prophet had erred faced possible charges of treason.

"I understand," I said, with a concerned nod, and tiptoed into my next question. "But what does he know of the location of the ark?"

The old man looked me in the eye for several moments and seemed about to speak when four young men burst into the room, shoved Williams to one side, and angrily halted the proceedings. One put a hand over the lens of Brad Houston's video camera; another started shouting at the old man. Ali leapt to his feet and held them at bay with both arms. The young men kept shouting and waving their hands at us to go. After a few moments of heated dialogue, Ali turned to me.

"We must leave," he announced. "They are not happy with our presence. We must leave quickly."

As the van pulled away and rumbled back down the road to Ardabil, my mind raced with thoughts of this strange countryside. I settled back and took a quick mental inventory. The similarities between these hills and the mysterious mountain Davis had detailed kept growing. I had just smelled, at Ghotor Suee, the rotten-egg odor he had described and had seen not just one, but many streams coming off the mountain. Sabalon, the tallest mountain north of Qazvin, still boasted a heavy crown of snow and ice, as Davis had reported. This mountain was the strongest candidate for where Ed Davis had seen his wooden object.

CHAPTER 15

UNDER ARREST AGAIN

We set off the following morning on a reconnaissance of the villages on the south side of the mountain. Each received us with great fanfare. Children and adults flocked around us with delighted enthusiasm, plying us with the ceremonial Muslim hospitality observed throughout the eastern hemisphere. At each stop, before we spoke a word about Noah's ark, the village patriarch typically ushered us into his domed tent or mud hut for a steaming pot of bitter tea, sweetened with small rocks of sugar held between the teeth.

I enjoyed these rituals, filled as they were with warm smiles and laughter. After each visit, Ali translated our heartfelt thanks for the kind hospitality. Here on the south side of the mountain, our questions about the ark inspired nothing but silence and blank stares. No one seemed to have any knowledge or oral traditions to share, in stark contrast to those on the north side, where lively histories of Noah's boat were nurtured.

Ali explained that villages on Sabalon's south side rarely socialized with those on the north, sharply reducing the cross-pollination of stories. I did notice that some villages featured the same multiple-terraced, stacked-adobe structures that I had seen in a photo of the village where Ed Davis said he had seen the old vineyard and ark artifacts. But no one we talked to had heard of Lors named Badi or Abas.

Arriving by mid-morning at our third village—a dusty mud-thatch settlement higher up the south-facing foothills—we accepted the now-expected invitation by the village patriarch to sit in his stucco bungalow for tea. Phil Trahern remained outside to check his global positioning system (GPS) coordinates. The next hour of idle conversation passed amiably, with questions about America, our families, and the reasons behind our visit to Iran.

The elder shook his head when asked about the ark. We were hearing no a lot in this area. Our conversation was interrupted by a commotion outside the hut. A Land Rover roared through the village gate and stopped a few feet from the elder's door. Three men in gray polyester suits and closely cropped beards stepped out and began barking questions at the villagers, who pointed them in our direction.

I smelled trouble and turned to Ali, whose face had grown cold and waxen. That's when I knew that our long-expected encounter with the Iranian secret police was taking place. Glancing about, I noticed Phil standing next to the van, looking tense and uncomfortable. I walked over and asked, "What's going on?"

He shrugged. "I don't know. Who are those guys?"

Ali hurried over and pulled me aside. "These villagers say that Mr. Trahern told them he was a pilot."

"A pilot?" I knew that the Iranians associated pilots and planes with the military, with espionage. I had discussed this very issue with the team beforehand. "Don't even hint at anything having to do with guns, war, or the military." I confronted Trahern about the statement and he denied making it, but a few minutes later another team member confirmed that Phil had, indeed, been boasting that he was a pilot.

Trahern had retreated to the van, slipping his GPS unit back in his pants' pocket as the police grilled Ali. After many emphatic gestures and pleas, Ali returned to the van, mumbling under his breath.

"Ali, what do they want?" I asked.

"They have ordered us to follow them back into Nir for questioning," he said. "Someone in this village called the police. We must go. Now!"

I glanced at Trahern, who conspicuously avoided my gaze, and gathered the team together.

"Stay calm, men," I said. "It looks as if we're about to see an Iranian police station up close."

We followed the Land Rover five miles out of the village, along a dusty jeep trail into Nir, a small desert town that welcomed visitors with a billboard reading "Allah is great! Down with the United States." When we had driven through Nir earlier that morning, Ali had been embarrassed by the sign and had tried to explain: "The people here like Americans. It is the government who puts up these signs."

"Remind me not to leave my business card at the Nir Chamber of Commerce," Larry Williams quipped from the back of the van.

The heavily guarded concrete and barbed-wire police compound sat at the center of town. By the time the police Land Rover turned into the gate, we had all managed to hide our video equipment, cameras, and Phil Trahern's GPS unit under seats, behind luggage, and inside our packs. A stout, bearded fellow that we assumed was the camp commander watched us from the guardhouse steps. He wore a rumpled military uniform with medals on the lapels and gravy stains on his chest pockets. When Ali stepped from the van, head hanging like a scolded pup, the scowling commander ordered him into the station.

Poor Ali, I thought, *living out his worst nightmare over our clumsy indiscretions.* We waited in the van.

Every twenty minutes or so, Ali—fussing and fretting—returned to the van with an update. "We don't have permission to be in this area," he kept saying, and then for good measure, "This puts my wife and my children in grave danger."

In the front of the van, our driver buried his head in his hands and said, "They are going to kill my family." I couldn't decide if these men really feared for their lives or if they just wanted to make us feel guilty.

"Ali, calm down," I said. "Just tell them I made you do it."

For two more hours, we waited inside the sweltering van, pondering our fate. We had not been charged with a crime, but being held against our will in a foreign country meant that we were actually under arrest. We had to act fast, because in Iran things can quickly turn sour.

Brad Houston asked Larry Williams for his satellite cell phone.

"I've got an idea," he said. "I could call NBC, or *Dateline,* back in the States, and tell my contacts we have a hostage situation here, that Americans are being held against their will. It may be our only chance."

"Give it a try," I said.

Repeated attempts to connect were unsuccessful. Larry Williams's cell phone couldn't pick up a signal inside the van, so we tried several times to stick his phone outside the window and dial the number, but guards kept walking by and he could never complete the call. I tried to divert the guard's attention by pretending to stretch my legs outside the van, but we never had enough time and finally gave up.

Bored to death and sick of waiting, Williams reached in his bag for a deck of cards and challenged me to a game of hearts.

"Deal me in," I said. We had played a few hands when Ali suddenly reemerged from the jail, the commander following close behind holding a snub-nosed revolver.

What's he going to do with that? I wondered, watching as he took out a single, chrome-plated bullet and tenderly loaded it into the chamber. For some reason, the image of Barney Fife came to mind. Ali leaned into the van and saw us playing cards.

"Oh no," he blurted. "Quickly! Hide them. It is illegal to play cards in Iran."

Without hesitating, we gathered them and tossed them over our shoulders, sending cards flying just as the commander poked his head in the van. Williams stepped on cards lying on the floor; I had cards stuffed down my shirt; Houston and Trahern sat on cards; cards were crammed under our seats and scattered in the aisle next to the cooler. We held our breath as the commander looked us over, then turned to Ali with another scolding. He rattled off a few angry sentences, frowned, looked us over once more, and then shook a final angry finger in our direction.

Ali turned, a shell-shocked expression on his face as he said, "We are free to go."

While it seemed inappropriate to cheer, we felt instant and profound relief. Ali barked at the driver, and we drove from the compound. We shared an unspoken sense of having received a conditional reprieve.

As our van sped past the outskirts of Nir toward Ardabil, Ali pulled me close. "They think you are CIA," he said, "or archaeologists here to steal our ancient treasures." Noting my puzzled expression, he explained, "Foreigners come to this region to dig for many ancient landmarks. They think you are here either to spy or to excavate the graves and altars at the top of Sabalon. I could not convince them that they were wrong. I said to them, 'You are crazy!'"

"Is that why they arrested us?" I asked.

"No," he said, nodding toward Phil. "The way Mr. Trahern talked about flying planes, the villagers feared he was up to something. Thinking he might be a soldier, they contacted the police."

"Perfect," I said. "So what does that mean for our trip?"

Ali sighed. "It means they will follow us from now on."

With that, our bad times in northwest Iran began.

We returned to Ardabil, where word of our arrest had spread. Since we had been detained by the secret police, we would now be treated as scorned intruders. From the favored ranks of welcome guests, we had passed, in a matter of hours, into the realm of despised untouchables.

Ali knew the routine, and we learned it soon enough. Wherever we went now, whether it was the hotel lobby or ordering meals at a restaurant, agents in dark polyester suits stopped and interrogated us. Out in the streets, we couldn't walk fifty feet without being halted by some young police sergeant and ordered to present our passports and visas. Even the desk manager at the Sabalon Hotel, kind and helpful the day before, was surly whenever we showed up in his lobby, and the porters either scowled or ignored us as we walked by. We never knew when the police would stop and browbeat us, and I knew that the longer we hung around, the worse it would get until we ended up in jail.

The way things stood, our chances of ever setting foot on Mount Sabalon looked poor indeed. At best, I figured, we had one more day to finish our business and get out of town. I called the team together.

"We've run out of time, men. We've got to get to Sabalon." Then I turned to Ali. "We want to climb the mountain. Take us there."

Wincing, he said, "We do not have permission."

"I understand. But it is compulsory that we climb the mountain."

SABALON RETREAT

Setting out early the next morning, we hired two young Kurdish drivers and instructed them to take us as high up Mount Sabalon as the roads would go. They agreed, and drove us in their battered 1960s model Land Rover through Sulfur City and along a narrow dirt road up the west saddle of Sabalon. For another two hours, we rocked and tilted along washed-out, rutted cart tracks, trying to ignore the sharp drop-offs on either side.

We reached a little stone hostel that sported medieval-looking brick spires on ruddy mud walls. Cut into the cliff side at about 12,000 feet, it seemed an adequately remote, inaccessible hideout offering temporary shelter from prying eyes. Ali said that it was constructed as a monastery during World War II, but that it was now a Muslim meditation retreat. It had ten stuffy, windowless rooms behind its heavy iron doors.

"We will be safe here for a time," Ali assured. "There are no phones and no villagers, and if you wish, you can climb the mountain from here."

At this altitude, we could feel the late September weather changing from fall to winter. As I strolled about the grounds with the frosty tundra crunching beneath my feet, I could see my breath and feel the icy nip of Caspian humidity stinging my fingertips. Twenty yards from the hostel was a popular trailhead frequented by local hikers and the occasional nomad, leading up a high ridge to the summit.

Mount Sabalon consists of 600 square miles of rugged foothills, serpentine ravines, and plunging gorges, any one of which might harbor a weather-beaten ship. From a certain perspective, the mountain appears to have a huge, solitary summit among smaller, rugged peaks, but scanned from other angles, this peak stretches into a range with four similarly sized summits in a row. *If Ed Davis climbed one of these peaks,* I thought, *the ark could be practically anywhere.*

We knew only that Badi and his brothers had taken Davis up a very hard, possibly forbidden route through hidden caves and extreme, rocky terrain to reach a ledge overlooking a massive gorge. By all accounts, that gorge lay hidden from view and received little or no foot traffic. I had no illusions that this handy footpath—no more than a quick tourist's trail to the top—would yield much information on Davis's route. Nonetheless, I wanted to climb it, hoping that by doing so I would at least gain a feel for the peak's vast topography.

Everyone in our group wanted to make the climb, but only Stuplich and I, fresh from Ararat's slopes, had come prepared with proper snow gear and climbing boots. I certainly hadn't expected to climb a mountain of this enormity in Iran. We had intended it strictly as a research trip, so the other members of the team had packed only light hiking gear. From the trailhead at 12,000 feet, it would take us eight hours to reach the 16,000-foot summit and return, a grueling stretch by any standard.

To quiet any grumbling, Stuplich pointed to a 500-foot rock face overlooking the trail.

"To reach the top from here," he said, "we would each have to climb the equivalent of eighteen of those." They stared at the cliff, a graphic picture of the effort and fortitude required to climb 4,000 near-vertical feet at high altitude. With the plunging temperature, it would be a punishing climb, even if we were properly outfitted. The sight of the cliff cooled the others to an ascent.

Less than a week after scaling Ararat, Stuplich and I stared up at another staggering peak, silently wondering what hardships it held for us. We returned to the hostel for a quick dinner and turned in early.

THE SUMMIT

Stuplich and I rose at 5:00 AM, strapped on our headlamps, put on gloves and warm clothes, tightened our boots, and hit the trail with our two Kurdish guides, who set a blistering pace. Having grown up in the local villages, they knew every little curve and turn in the rock, and they galloped up the trail like mountain goats.

Still nursing bone-deep aches and muscle fatigue from Turkey, Stuplich and I quickly realized that we were in for another punishing workout. I took several deep breaths and told Stuplich, "Don't worry about me, Bob. I'll make it." He nodded, and we set off in breathless pursuit of the wiry Kurds.

The Sabalon trail rose nearly straight up a narrow, stair-step terrace of rocky switchbacks—the antithesis of Mount Ararat's marathoner's grade—and shot us directly into a dense cloud bank. Over the next four lung-searing hours, we rose 4,000 feet on the surprisingly well-groomed trail that finally emptied into a tight, windswept plateau framed by granite cliffs and cloven glaciers. Here we stood a mere fifty yards below the summit, but having climbed so fast and so high without rest, my heart hammered in a heavy and irregular way that I had never felt before. Even after resting for several minutes and trying to relax and let my pulse settle, I couldn't catch my breath. *Have I pushed it too far?* I wondered. *After all these years and hard ascents, is my old ticker now about to blow a gasket?* In time, the locomotive heartbeat quieted, but my breath never fully recovered while we stayed on the summit.

We stood beside a beautiful aquamarine lake, set gently into the plateau like a milky opal. Its pristine waters would have served us well four days earlier, descending Ararat, and I was surprised to see it up so high. Chunks of ice from the glacier sat half-submerged at the water's edge.

The temperature had dropped to well below freezing. The sky was wild and turbulent as dense patches of purple-black clouds alternately wet our faces and bathed the summit in stark, strobe-like splashes of brilliant light. Ice crystals formed on our unshaven faces, and when I took out my video camera, I discovered its batteries had frozen. Stuplich tried to snap a picture, but the shutter of his Nikon had iced shut. With stiff, numb fingers, I fumbled in my pack to retrieve another set of batteries and at length managed to replace the frozen ones. My video camera whirred to life, allowing me to record the arctic tableau.

The summit sat just above us, but the exhausted Kurds, quaking from the cold and dressed only in thin nylon jackets, lightweight gloves, khaki pants, and tennis shoes, motioned for us to go on. I feared that they might freeze or suffer frostbite, but they didn't seem concerned. As Stuplich and I climbed on, treading past a wintry Stonehenge of towering, heavily icicled boulders, I turned to see the Kurds curled next to one another beneath a small ledge, warming themselves like cats beside a fire.

"We've got to hurry," I shouted at Stuplich, fighting to stand in the teeth of a fierce, freezing wind. "Bad weather is coming in."

Within minutes, we had scaled the final ice-glazed pinnacle, hoping for better visibility, but the clouds grew too thick and blustery for us to see anything of the range below. We could barely see our own feet.

Beside us, the wind had cut the ice into horizontal spikes on the rock, like shark's teeth stuck in granite. Turning to Stuplich, I shouted, "That's our cue to leave."

Before leaving, I took a moment to stare into the intensifying whiteout, trying to imagine the curvature and shape of the lower bowls and ravines and wanting to project myself into that wet, sleety canyon of 1943 where Ed Davis and Badi might have passed.

I could not; the mountain would not allow it. We could barely stand on the ice-blasted summit.

"Let's head down!" Stuplich yelled through howling gusts, and I knew that we had to go. It took us three hours to scramble down the trail to the hostel, where hot tea and rice warmed us. Another year of dreams and clues would pass before I had the privilege of standing on this awesome peak again.

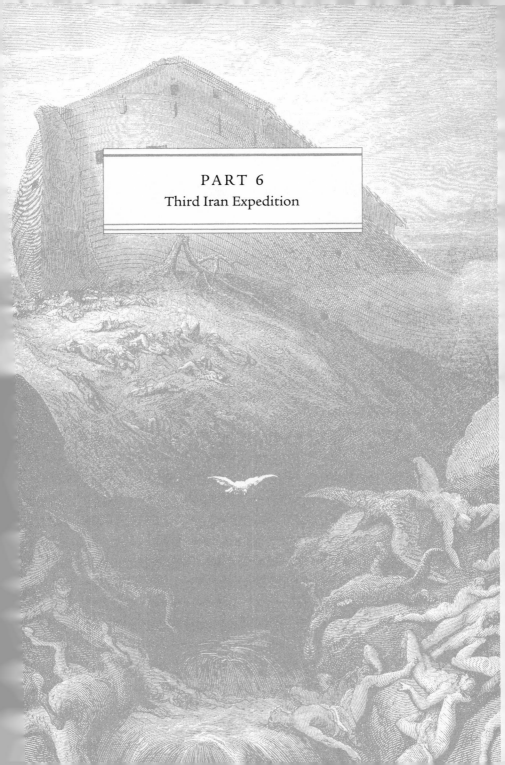

PART 6
Third Iran Expedition

CHAPTER 16

THE MAP, THE SEAL, AND THE "OBJECT"

Mount Sabalon, Iran, July 2000

On April 20, 1999, the heart of the nation broke when two gunmen entered a Littleton, Colorado, high school and made it the scene of the deadliest school shooting in American history. Twelve students and one teacher lost their lives that day; twenty-three others were injured.

I live in Colorado Springs, just over fifty miles from where the massacre occurred. I watched the news stories, read the articles, and learned something about the lives of those slain and wounded.

I learned, for instance, that Rachel Scott, among the first to die in a hail of bullets on the school lawn, had a tender heart for the misfits and social outcasts at her school. This beautiful seventeen-year-old was an outspoken Christian, with gifts for writing poetry and acting. What I didn't know until I met her father is that she had a prophetic sense of her imminent death. Believing that her life would be cut short before her prime, she had set about to touch those she saw floundering on Columbine's fringes. In the weeks before the shootings, Rachel shared her faith with Dylan Klebold and Eric Harris, not realizing that her act of courage would make her a high-priority target.

I learned that another victim, sixteen-year-old John Tomlin, also loved the Lord. At just fourteen, John had talked himself into a job so he could save for a truck. He had his eye on a career in the military. John also had a heart for life's outcasts and underdogs, as I learned when I talked with his father. He took up their cause at every opportunity. John Tomlin lost his life in the school library while doing his homework.

As I have shared my adventures at churches and rallies across the country, it has been a great privilege to meet some of the parents of these precious young people. Darrell Scott and John Tomlin Sr.—the fathers of Rachel and John—have become close friends.

I met Darrell at a conference in Wichita, Kansas, shortly after he left a lucrative career to launch Chain Reaction, an evangelistic, anti-violence ministry to teens. I saw in Darrell a reserved, humble man of serious intellect, trained as a theologian but loving to laugh, play golf, and tell jokes.

People say that John Tomlin comes across as a gentle, soft-spoken bear of a man—and he does—but I could still see the pain of his terrible loss lingering just below the surface. John shares Darrell's vision for reaching teens with a message of hope through Christ.

Our paths kept crossing on the conference-speaking circuit, and we spent time together, having lunch or seeing a movie, sharing our lives and talking about God and his purposes. But too much talk of Columbine wearied them. They spent the better part of every day discussing the minute details of the tragedy. Our discussions inevitably turned to my travels, chasing after lost arks and holy mountains. Their eyes would light up while listening to these wild stories and change them from somber men into schoolboys on the edge of high adventure.

When I described my plans to return to Iran to continue searching for Noah's ark, they asked me to take them along. Their enthusiasm blessed me, and I promised that I would think about it. But truthfully, I didn't feel very optimistic about it. I get many requests—sometimes as many as ten per day—from people asking me to take them on an adventure. It seems that everyone from Fortune 500 executives bored with life to little old ladies wanting to get out of the house are dying to put their lives at risk.

Yet the more I pored over our maps and planned the stages of our itinerary, the more I realized that this might not be as harsh a trip as I had imagined. If we could take four-wheel-drive vehicles to within a couple of miles of the target, we wouldn't have to hike for days across the high plains or endure endless hours of technical climbing while scaling high cliffs and crossing deadly boulder fields. That meant that I might be able to take some friends—who needed a break but might not have the necessary skills or physical conditioning for climbing—on a once-in-a-lifetime adventure.

I finally thought, *Why not?* Whatever risks we might face couldn't possibly outweigh the fun and diversion such a trip would give to John and Darrell, who had spent the past year immersed in the horror of Columbine. I called them to say, "If you still want to go, mail me your passports for the visa applications!"

THE TEAM

Now I had to settle on the rest of the team. Our navigator would be Dan Toth, an ex-Navy SEAL who had contacted me several months before and volunteered his services. I hoped that his experience using a handheld global positioning system and topographical maps would guide us up the maze of trails on Sabalon. Next, I invited my brother Paul, who had traveled with me to Turkey, and David Halbrook, coauthor of my previous books and a Christian brother with whom I've become close friends. I rounded out the team with Todd Phillips, a youth pastor from Austin, Texas; Larry Williams, my adventurous old friend; and Dick Bright, the bulldog of ark searchers.

When we arrived in Iran again, Ali told me some surprising news over lunch. "Mr. Bob, I have found some news that might be of interest," he said, casually informing us that he had been doing some research on Mount Sabalon.

I had asked him in advance to locate a few books about the mountain, but I didn't expect what he had found. Beginning with a short history lesson on Mount Sabalon from an Iranian perspective, his first news was about the mountain's legacy as the birthplace of Zoroaster, one of Iran's revered prophets.

Zoroaster set the tone for Persia's early spiritual temperament and founded Zoroastrianism, one of the world's oldest religions that influences much of Iranian art, architecture, and philosophy. Though its social impact has diminished in the Islamic state, Zoroaster is still revered by locals as one of the first prophets to teach about an omnipotent, invisible god. Zoroaster is symbolized in ancient rock reliefs by fire and is still worshipped in Zoroastrian temples in the form of "eternally" burning flames.

"Yes?" I wasn't sure what Ali was getting at.

In his halting English, Ali replied, "I have found a book by a famous Iranian scholar, Professor Poordavood, who confirms that Zoroaster was born in Iranian Azerbaijan. Professor Poordavood cites ancient texts attesting that during Zoroaster's lifetime, Mount Sabalon was known as 'Var-Jam-Kard.'"

"Okay," I said, still missing the connection. "What does *Var-Jam-Kard* mean?"

"I'm sorry," said Ali, embarrassed. "*Var-Jam-Kard* comes from the Old Persian, the ancient Zoroastrian language. *Var-Jam-Kard* means 'Noah's Mountain.'"

David Halbrook and I stared at each other, our expressions registering astonishment.

"Mount Sabalon was once known as Noah's Mountain?" David asked. "Tell us, Ali, when did Zoroaster live?"

Ali explained that Professor Poordavood had been attempting to prove that Zoroaster lived as far back as 4,000 years ago, though the best scholarly estimates tell us that he lived between 638 BC and 551 BC. Even so, the title "Var-Jam-Kard" for Mount Sabalon was one of the oldest known references associating Noah with a specific mountain.

"If what you're saying is true," David said, "it introduces a new timetable for one of the first mountains named for Noah." (We later investigated all references to verify Ali's claims, and each checked out.) Brightened by our enthusiasm, Ali said, "There is more."

"What is it?" I asked.

"We've always thought the original capital of Urartu was situated near Lake Van in Turkey. The Urartian Empire dates to about 1400 BC and died out in about 600 BC. According to a famous Iranian scholar—Dr. Abdul Hussein Zarinkub—the first capital of Urartu carved its foothold in the region of Lake Urmia in Iran in the first millennium BC."

Ali paused, then added, "Only later did the Urartian rulers move the capital west to a city near Lake Van in Turkey, called Torvashbeh."

I didn't know it then, but the esteemed British historian David M. Rohl agreed with Dr. Zarinkub: "The later kingdom of Urartu [Ararat] was originally located here [east of Lake Urmia] in its early days, before shifting its heartland to the area around Lake Van."[1]

Pondering Ali's data while sipping my soda, I casually mentioned to him that in 30 BC, Nicholas of Damascus wrote of the ark as coming to rest on a mountain "above the Minyas in Armenia."

"The Minyas?" Ali echoed, well versed in that region's ethnic origin. "*Minyas* corresponds to the Minni tribes, who lived in the region south and east of Lake Urmia in northwest Iran. So . . . what mountain did Mr. Nicholas mean?"

"Well," I said, "the tallest mountain in the region above the Minyas is Mount Sabalon."

"Ah," he said, thumbing through his notes. "Everything seems to be pointing to Mount Sabalon." He looked up. "That is good, no?"

It was good, but I would later come to know that other tall mountains in the region also fit the designation of "above the Minyas." In any event, it was boding well for an Iranian location of the mountains of Ararat.

❦

Dan Toth struggled to find the road that would take us up Mount Sabalon. We had done little more than drive around in circles, trying to find the right rutted dirt path toward the summit. We had a target object at about 12,000 feet that Dan, the ex-Navy SEAL, had identified in a satellite photo. Also, Dr. Ed Holroyd, a professor of atmospheric science and physical research for the Remote Sensing and Geographic Information Group of the U.S. Bureau of Reclamation had conditionally endorsed this object as possibly being man-made. Dr. Holroyd, however, was cautious, assigning a seventy-five percent chance that the object was an anomaly. Dan Toth had done an enormous amount of work nailing down the location of his site, and he said he could get us there using a handheld GPS. The canyon he had identified looked like the terrain where Ed Davis might have been, he said. It fit the contours that Davis had described so vividly, but finding it in this enormous mountain range had become a tedious chore.

The morning had turned into an endless series of starts and stops, false reads, and blind alleys; we would turn down a road that seemed headed in the right direction, but after a mile or two, we would come to an unexpected fork or dead end. We would stop, turn back, and ask the locals where we had gone wrong and which way we needed to go. They would send us off on a new path, and the maddening cycle would repeat itself.

Through it all, we remained in full view of the humpback ridge near the summit, but we could never seem to stay on course. Just when it seemed that we might span a rise and come face-to-face with our prize, the road would end and leave us stranded on another dead-end plateau.

Ali and Dan wrestled with maps and argued with our drivers about routes that didn't exist. At every stop, they huddled with a nameless succession of nomads, village chieftains, and ruddy young shepherd boys. Despite the harried dialogues, no one had much help to offer. Off we would drive, up the next ragged goat path spiraling into the next towering succession of lethal switchbacks, until once again, the road ended or vanished into a field of clover, leaving us no closer to the prize than when we started.

And so it went. When Dan and Ali hustled out the maps, the rest of us stretched our legs, staged impromptu rock-throwing contests, snapped a few photos of the rugged hills, the occasional goat, or a grazing camel, or simply admired the majestic sweep of Sabalon's roller-coaster lowlands. Then Dan would shout, "Let's go!" and we'd pile back into the cramped, dusty Land Rovers and backtrack down the road, grinding gears up another new sheep path. Dan had purchased ten-year-old Russian maps of the plain of Sabalon at a reputable map store in Colorado. But in the Middle East, the smartest-looking maps often have little in common with the actual terrain. Our maps illustrated roads that had fallen into disuse or might never have existed. Looking at the actual terrain, I found it a stretch to think that any of these miserable camel trails had found their way onto an actual map. They were little more than wispy tire tracks breaking dirt through stands of tumbleweed.

After stopping at several nomad camps for directions, we eventually passed 12,000 feet and were close to the target area. We had crossed a small stream high above the valley when another crisis hit. Our drivers had stopped alongside the stream to fill their radiators when I realized that our two-day supply of food had mysteriously dwindled. Checking our provisions, I found only a few bottles of water, a loaf and a half of bread, and a couple of cans of tuna to feed ten men. Somehow, all our food had disappeared.

"How did that happen?" I asked the team. I was bewildered. All day we had just been nibbling on personal stashes of PowerBars, nuts, and trail mix. I turned to Ali, who wore a doleful expression. "Ali, do you know?"

Wringing his hands, he said, "I am sorry, Mr. Bob." He confessed that he had overestimated our provisions and had given our food to a series of guides and drivers at each stop.

I pulled him aside so as not to embarrass him. "Why did you give away our food?"

Slapping his forehead, he tried to explain. "They were very hungry. They had nothing else to eat."

"But now we don't have enough food," I replied.

The supplies I had bought to last us through the night and the following day were almost gone. We couldn't turn back now to buy more. We had driven five hours into the foothills and finally had the target zone squarely in our sights. We felt too close. No, I decided, there would be no turning back tonight.

At first I wanted to scold Ali, but quickly recognized that he had acted out of compassion. So I steered the conversation elsewhere. We still hadn't climbed above sheep country. Wherever we turned, we passed another shepherd's camp, with grazing flocks nearby. It gave me an idea.

"Ali," I said, "what about these nomad camps? Can we buy food from one of them? Do you think they would sell us a sheep?"

It seemed a rational request, given our circumstances—simply to buy a sheep and pay them whatever they asked to cook it for us. Surely someone up here would sell us a sheep.

Ali pondered it a moment and then said with a clap of his hands, "You have money? No problem. We can buy food."

I called the team together. By now, we were quite a sight—hot and gamy, tired and hungry, ready to throw down a sleeping bag, build a campfire, and spend a night on the mountain. We had been bouncing in the backs of jeeps so long our kidneys ached.

"We're not going back tonight, men," I said. "Tonight, we live off the fat of the land."

TARGET FOUND

In the waning light of dusk, we crested the final high ridge of a peak just west of Sabalon's towering summit and parked our caravan. We tumbled out on the green tundra and stretched our legs on a mildly sloping plateau near an abandoned shepherd's camp. To the west, we could see an oblique, deep blue tract of snow-spattered mountains and sinewy ravines.

Dan walked over to the ridgeline, took out his GPS, and stared into the first rays of a brooding sunset. Two miles off stood a giant, dome-shaped knuckle of granite, hunkered claw-like over a range of high mountain meadows. If our estimates were correct, this tangle of granite overlooked the deep yawning gorge. Dan pointed toward the huge cleft of fractured granite and cried, "That's it! We're here!"

We had made it, but at so late an hour that I felt more relief than joy. The gorge sat two, maybe three miles away, an easy hike with backpacks. But it would have to wait until morning. Hungry, tired, and thirsty, we had to secure our accommodations for the night. Driving up the pass, I had noticed a small shepherd's encampment tucked into a beautiful, bowl-shaped meadow, with a large flock of sheep grazing peacefully on the ridge above.

"Let's go eat!" I said, as we climbed back into the Land Rovers and coasted back into the valley, praying that we might find food and a place to pitch our tents for the night. If all went well, we would complete our journey in the morning, climb the mile or two up and over a towering hogs' back butte, and stare down into Davis Canyon. It was the moment of truth.

Now, I wondered, *how would our hosts below receive this unlikely crew of hungry Americans?*

LOW ON THE MOUNTAIN

The young boy raised his rifle and fired into the air, a signal to his father, still tending flocks on the mountainside, to hurry down.

We had arrived at the sheep camp with all the subtlety of a traveling circus—three dirty, overheated Land Rovers piled with packs and large, unshaven strangers. From their perspective, I doubted that our entrance had made a good impression, but Ali went straight to work tendering our proposal. He represented a team of American explorers searching for a valuable artifact from history; we had government approval to be on the mountain; we were hungry, and, if they agreed, we would buy a sheep from them, price no object; and for an additional fee, they would slaughter and cook our meal. Then, at the going rate, we would pitch our tents just outside their camp for the night; in the morning, we would climb the mountain, attend to our business, break camp, and be gone by evening.

From the looks on their faces, it was an unusual request. David Halbrook had an interesting take on it: "Imagine coming home at the end of a long day to a group of pushy, unwashed Iranians standing in your driveway. They ask to spend the night in your backyard, and, by the way, they are hungry and would like to eat one of your dogs, which they will pay you to kill and cook for their dinner. Price is no object!"

In such a light, our proposal seemed crude and preposterous. We laughed at the absurdity of it, but after several minutes of lively negotiations, Ali struck a deal with the young shepherd. Since his father hadn't yet returned, he and his brothers selected a fine, healthy-looking sheep for us. They brought it to us, and we took turns holding the beast—smelly, kicking, and bleating—in our arms, trying to determine its weight. I had no idea what a pound of mutton went for on Mount Sabalon, but Ali finally negotiated a price of thirty-five dollars for the whole animal, minus the pelt. The boys ran off to build a fire.

We unloaded the trucks and chose our tent sites with a building sense of excitement. With our accommodations secured, thoughts returned to the mission at hand. Our camp sat in the shadow of a towering ridge cresting over the lip of a canyon, below which, Dan assured us, sat a dreadful gorge known as Davis Canyon.

"Bob and I will have to rappel down with ropes and pitons," he said, implying that the rest of the team would watch from above. From there, he said, we would see the ark, broken in two and jutting from the gorge, partially concealed under two prongs of talus and scree. "It's right over that rise," he insisted to anyone within earshot, deaf to my suggestion that he temper his remarks. "I've never been more confident of anything in my life."

I rolled my eyes but didn't say anything. He obviously had a severe case of ark fever.

I turned east. Mount Sabalon's angry purple tips stared down at me as its row of spines towered above us. The Bible said that the ark came to rest on the mountains of Ararat, and as the waters began to recede, the tops of the surrounding peaks became visible (Genesis 8:5). I looked up at those lofty peaks and felt, or really hoped, that we had found the mountains of Ararat.

But as I inspected our campsite from far below those imposing crags, I thought, *This camp of ours rests in a high meadow, not high on the summit. It's just not high enough. Flocks and children scamper carefree among the hills. Sheep encampments dominate these glades. If the ark sits just over the ridge, as Dan insists that it does, these people should know about it. But Ali has already asked them, and no one here has ever seen or heard of the boat that inspired Ed Davis to say, "You won't believe how big it is!"*

I recalled that Davis had talked about steep canyons and dangerous gorges, about sheer, dangling trails and ropes they had to use to tie themselves together, of having to claw up craggy cliffs and traverse ice-covered ledges for several days.

Dangerous cliffs? Ice-capped ledges? I saw nothing of the kind in the scenery around us. A creeping disappointment began to set in. I had trusted the experts who had so enthusiastically endorsed this area of the mountain as being Ed Davis's site, but it was nothing like what Davis had described to me.

In hindsight—and in fairness to the experts—I realize that satellite images are a lot like looking down at the top of someone's head from high above. You don't know what the person really looks like until you get down to eye level. Each of the facets Dan pointed out as corresponding to Davis's map remained deeply compelling. The evidence and scholarly opinions had left us no choice but to come and see it in person. But here, at eye level, our target left much to be desired. I tried to remain optimistic, but at that moment my heart said that our target zone sat too low on the mountain.

CHAPTER 17

THE BLOOD OF THE LAMB

The temperature dropped dramatically as the sun ducked behind the mountains, and the chilly breeze sent us to our packs for jackets and sweaters. The shepherd boys called us over to a tripod of lashed logs where they had stacked wood for a fire and tethered the sheep we had purchased for our dinner. They had hobbled its front legs with leather straps so that it knelt involuntarily as if in prayer, head bowed to one side. I imagined that its eyes had a sad cast to them, as if it knew what was coming. It knelt before us, the picture of meekness—not struggling, but silent. It was the meekest creature I had ever seen.

The sight of the poor animal hobbled before us quelled the frivolity of our campout and turned the mood somber. Todd Phillips and Darrell Scott stood over the sheep, running cold hands through its dense wool, perhaps intending to comfort it. Until then, we hadn't given it a second thought, but the sight of an animal awaiting slaughter unsettled us. What had we expected? Dinner served to us on a silver tray, dressed and sizzling, as in a restaurant? To our hosts, this ritual was a daily routine, as common as any other task. To us, presiding over the slaughter of a living creature so that we could eat was a foreign experience. None of us knew how we felt about it.

We stood together in a quiet circle as the lad walked over, put an arm around the sheep's head, and calmly laid a blade to its neck. Before he could make the fatal slash, I shouted, "Wait!" Startled and confused, he stopped and looked around.

"Give us a minute, please," Dick Bright chimed in. "We must pray first."

Bright cupped his hands under his chin to help the lad understand. We had already decided to formalize our prayer for this momentous meal. We had been extremely fortunate to find the target zone among the baffling hills and roads and felt blessed to have met these hospitable nomads. We wanted to consecrate the meal to the Lord and offer it up, after the manner of the Israelites, as a thank offering.

As the boy pulled back to the outskirts of our circle, we joined hands around the bound sheep. Bright led us.

"Lord," he began, "we thank you for this wonderful adventure, for these gracious nomads, and for these great brothers. More than that, we thank you for loving us even when we didn't love you, and for dying in our stead. We thank you, Father, for this gentle, fettered lamb, who like your Son has laid down its life so that we might live. As it says in Isaiah, Jesus was oppressed and afflicted, yet he did not open his mouth; he was led like a lamb to the slaughter, and as a sheep before its shearers is silent, so he did not open his mouth.

"So, Lord," he continued, "we give you honor and praise and present to you this gentle animal as a burnt offering, that you might receive it as a sweet fragrance of our love. And we receive it back from you—as we have your Son in our hearts—to give us strength and sustenance for our trials ahead. In thanksgiving and praise to your holy name, we pray. Amen."

Bright's stirring prayer, delivered with a depth of feeling I hadn't expected and so appropriate to the drama playing before us, captured the kaleidoscope of emotions coursing through me. Hobbled before us lay perhaps the truest picture of Jesus I had ever encountered—a gentle lamb, a living sacrifice bound on an altar, and silent before its executioner. The gravity of the moment stole my breath.

I looked at the others. Everyone was quiet. The boy walked back over and, in one smooth motion, reached down and made a deep slit across the sheep's throat. A violent spurt of blood shot ten feet across the meadow. The animal dropped to its stomach, supported by the boy's steadying hands. David and Paul turned away and walked up the slope to the tents, unable to watch. The rest of us remained, jaws clenched, watching a life bleed out before our eyes.

"It's the nomad way . . . how they live and survive," I kept telling myself, thinking that normalizing the ritual might lessen its sting. Killing a sheep this way seems as normal for them as buying cellophane-wrapped hamburger at the grocery store is for us. Every day, thousands of animals are killed to feed hungry humans. It is normal, nothing new or unique.

Then why did it move me so?

I had seen the same ritual acted out time and again in my travels, but always as a sideline observer, watching someone else's exotic customs, never as a needy, hungry recipient having to slaughter a lamb for survival. Yet here I stood, hungry, out of my element, and by any measure, in need. The lamb was heaving its last, quivering breaths.

Dan Toth spoke first. "A lamb is the only animal that doesn't cry out when it's dying," he said, matter-of-factly. He pulled on his gloves because the temperature continued to drop.

Again, I thought of Jesus, how he had stood silent before his jury, quietly endured his beatings, refused to defend himself, and finally, suffered an agonizing death on a cross. I glanced about the circle; did the others catch this piercing allegory?

The sheep's body went slack, its breathing ended. It died quietly, but the agony and desperation of its final swoon had been painfully real, just as Jesus' agony erupted in a final, desperate cry: "My God, why have you forsaken me?"

The boys cut off the animal's head, then began massaging the carcass to drain the rest of the blood. About five feet from the spreading crimson pool, they skinned and butchered it as if they were peeling a potato.

The silence in our group was palpable. Darrell Scott and John Tomlin stood side by side, transfixed by the rustic passion play. One could only imagine what was going through their minds.

One thing I knew was that our team would not go hungry tonight. We would have our meat for dinner, and it would come at the price of an unforgettable memory.

FEAST OF THE LAMB

The elder shepherd, trailing two huge Kangal dogs with spiked collars, returned to camp. Apprised by his sons of the nature of our visit, he cheerfully began to supervise the cooking chores. Through it all, I watched Ali maintain a close vigil on all that was happening. He was dog tired and dirty, his face unshaven and his eyes at half-mast—he looked completely frazzled and strung out. We had run him ragged.

As Americans in Iran, we were babes in the woods, unable to speak the native language and ill-equipped to manage our own affairs. As our de facto babysitter, Ali translated every question, negotiated every transaction, changed our money, bought our groceries, saw to it that our laundry was properly washed, ran every errand, and made every phone call for nine grown men. Over the past two days, Ali had mediated every turn and pass up the slope, tried to make sense of the maps and roads, and dealt minute by minute with Dan and a rotating cast of guides. I knew that he hadn't slept more than a few hours since he picked us up at the Tehran airport four days earlier. Yet he never complained, never even raised an eyebrow as we pressed him on all sides. He just kept displaying his punchy, overtired grin, doing his best to make our every wish his urgent command.

Now, at a point in the trip when no one would have noticed or blamed him for ducking into a Land Rover and catching a quick nap, he managed the butchering and cooking chores, barking soft orders and sticking his nose into the thick of things. With finicky care, he supervised the cleaning and cubing of the meat, skewered it himself, and even instructed the shepherd boys on how to stir the coals so it didn't scorch the kebabs. He made sure that everything was properly prepared and grilled to perfection.

From my last trip to Iran, I knew Ali to be energetic, competent, and willing to serve, but I hadn't realized until this remarkable display what a thoroughly undeserved gift we had been given in this small, humble man.

When the elder shepherd tried to scoop the sizzling meat into a cold metal basin, Ali stopped him. "No, no, no!" he scolded. "It will get cold. Bring me a basket of hot flat bread."

The boys sprinted off across the field and returned minutes later with a steaming platter of fresh-baked, paper-thin flat bread. With great care, Ali wrapped the pieces of meat inside several layers of bread and covered the whole affair with clean white linen. He carried the steaming bundle, nuzzled in his arms like a baby, up the hill to our campsite and laid it tenderly on a large blanket at our feet. Ravenous, we watched Ali unwrap the linen cloth and unfold the bread, releasing a cloud of savory steam that filled the air with a spit-roasted aroma. Before us was a sumptuous feast—seven pounds of sizzling, flame-seared, prime cuts.

Children arrived minutes later with fresh goat cheese and home-made yogurt in silver serving bowls, and then brought up a steaming pot of tea. With rumbling stomachs, we took turns handpicking our cuts, wrapping the lightly charred chunks in sheets of flat bread like a giant burrito, and ladling on the goat cheese and yogurt. For the next forty minutes we stood laughing and eating, scarcely making a dent in the delectable, satisfying meal.

A lovely sweetness had drifted back into our midst. Out of the evening's heaviness came a spirit of levity and companionship. Camping above the timberline in mountains few Westerners had seen, enjoying the company of a rare group of men, and relishing each bite of a priceless meal had ushered in a depth of fellowship and open feeling that few of us knew back home, submerged in our busy lives.

Still, the weight of the day's events had made an impression upon us. In frosty darkness, we strolled down to the fire pit and lingered about the campfire. We were so high on the mountain that firewood was scarce, but our generous hosts tossed what looked to be their last logs on the blaze, just for our pleasure. The mountain air grew colder by the minute, so we huddled closer to the warmth, sipping hot tea from dainty cups among the grinning, chattering nomads, and squeezing the marrow from the moment.

In the quiet, Todd Phillips cleared his throat as if to speak. He seemed perfectly at home among these cheery nomads. Within an hour of our arrival, he had quickly made friends with the youngsters, gathering them about like nieces and nephews, teaching them martial arts tricks, and even riding one of their horses bareback up the ridge. His face shone bright in the firelight as he addressed us with a quiet smile.

"I just want to thank you all for letting me tag along," he began, his subtle Texas twang flavoring his words. "I've been thinking about the ark. But I know that whether we find it or not, this night alone has made the trip worth it for me. The trip has taught me something about myself. The act of stepping on a plane in the United States and flying halfway around the world to search for Noah's ark—believing in my heart that it really, truly exists, based simply on what God said in his Word—has become one of the most significant acts of my life."

He paused, dabbed at an eye, then added, "What does that mean? Standing here around this fire with all you guys will allow me to go

back home and minister God's Word in a fresh new way to a lost and
. . ." He checked the quaver in his voice, then proceeded. "It allows
me to go back and minister to a lost, incredibly damaged, and pessi-
mistic section of our youth in a way that will change their hearts."

He glanced my way. "As far as I'm concerned, regardless of what
we do or don't find over that ridge tomorrow, this entire trip has
already been an absolute success. It has been my rejuvenation. I
can't fully explain it, but just finding this meadow has energized
me like no other time in my life."

Everyone smiled—even some of the nomads—and nodded softly
in agreement. The fire had burned down to embers. No one wanted
to leave. With the last dying sparks spiraling into the air, we talked
quietly, stretching the moment as long as possible. Nomad children stood close by, serving us piping hot tea with rocks of sugar—
simply, it seemed, to be near us. Our presence seemed to give them
a vague cause for celebration.

As the biting chill drove us one by one to our tents, I stayed for a
minute longer, staring at the stars in the vast, ebony expanse. And
that's when my flash of revelation hit me.

Scanning the heavens and replaying each stage of the trip in my
mind, I suddenly knew why I had spent almost two weeks riding in
planes and vans and jeeps, cramped and uncomfortable, bouncing
across a rugged wilderness in suffocating heat, to reach this half-
acre of paradise. Certainly we had found undeniable evidence to
support our theses about the ark. I believed, beyond a shadow of a
doubt, that we had found the lost mountains of Ararat and now
camped at the foot of a peak where Noah's ark most likely came to
rest. And while the consequences of that alone exceeded anything I
could fathom, I had stumbled unwittingly upon treasure of a

deeper kind. Something about this moment, these guys, and this experience had opened my heart to a subtle discovery far greater than I could have hoped for.

To my left, Darrell Scott spoke in thoughtful whispers to Larry Williams about life and its purpose, forgiveness, and the love it took for God to send his only Son, an innocent Lamb, to die for us. Larry listened carefully, nodding in agreement and asking questions. We had come here as a team, and as a team, it seemed, our thoughts had shifted from the physical to the spiritual, from raw adventure to something truly miraculous.

Until that moment I hadn't fully seen it. I hadn't fully understood what I had lost, traveling the world, giving it my all and trying my best to point others to the Savior. Hurrying along on my ministry treadmill, I had remained sharply disciplined, focused on who Jesus is and why he lived and died. I knew well the details of Christ's birth, death, and resurrection. Amid the clamor, I could "Jesus talk" with the best.

But slowly, steadily, I had lost something. Over the years, I had visited so many churches that they all looked alike, and I had heard so many messages that the simple, unadorned truth of Christ had become blurred and diluted. Somewhere along the line, the Bible got wrapped in cellophane, the church packaged in Styrofoam.

Through the busyness and chaos of life, through my own globe-trotting wanderlust, searching for emblems that should have kept my heart fixed and fervent, the pain, the anguish, the miracle, and the ecstasy of the Gospel had become a mere Sunday school lesson, a slice of dry curriculum. It had lost its immediacy, its power. But here, on a chilly, windswept mountain in northwest Iran, I had watched the blade make its cut; I had seen and smelled the blood and found it a harsh remedy for our needy condition.

My thoughts flashed to the harshness of sin in our lives and to the extreme remedy that had been required—an innocent Lamb, butchered in my place, saving me, transforming me, and giving me the strength and sustenance to go on. On a night in which even the bracing breeze seemed to speak of these matters, God restored in me the joy of my salvation. Surrounded by friends and confronted by the meekness of a dying lamb, he reintroduced me to his Son.

Such a spiritual awakening could have happened nowhere else for me. I had come looking for an ark, with its decayed footings and wooden timbers, but on a bristly cold, pristine night on Mount Sabalon, God chose to reveal his Son yet again, and my eyes were opened afresh.

GOOD NIGHT, SABALON

Sabalon loomed above us, a stoic, black pyramid framed by the light of a full moon. Behind us stood the tall, slender ridge we would climb in the morning, to find whatever lay beyond. I had no idea exactly what that was, but I knew what I hoped for.

I stared at the brooding red moon hanging high in the south and heard David Halbrook talking to Dick Bright by our tent. I could hear the excitement in his voice as he wrestled to put words to his own clarified insights.

"To have the opportunity to experience a night like this," he whispered, "and still to have even a remote expectation of walking over that ridge in the morning and, just possibly, seeing the remains of Noah's ark. It just seems so . . ." He trailed off.

"Blessed?" Bright replied, completing the sentence. "Yes, I agree, we are blessed. And whatever happens tomorrow, we can rest assured that God led us to this mountain for a purpose."

By now suspecting that God had led me here, at least in part, to hear those very words, I strolled back toward our tent. Darrell Scott walked up from the campfire to join me. I could tell from the intense look in his eyes that he had something important to say, but his voice was so soft and distant that I asked him to speak up.

He smiled and said, "I just wanted to tell you that I've named this valley 'Rachel's Valley' in memory of my daughter. You might not know that Rachel's name means 'God's little lamb.'"

I listened, quietly amazed, as he described how the sacrifice of the lamb had dialed up such a profound sadness that for a few agonizing moments he didn't know if he could bear it. Strangely enough, he emerged from his grief to a new strength and resolve.

Glancing back at the ruby patch of blood-stained hillside still shining in the moonlight, he continued, "I can't fully explain the symbolic impact of that moment, but . . . a few weeks before the shootings, Rachel had performed for the Columbine talent show a pantomime titled 'Watch the Lamb.' In it, she acted out the passion and crucifixion of Christ."

His gaze was distant, fixed on a faraway memory. "Watching that sheep die today," he said, "reminded me of something I read in Rachel's journal shortly after she was killed." He took a deep breath and said, "She had begun to share her faith boldly at school. She had even recently witnessed to Eric Harris and Dylan Klebold, but in the process, had begun to feel rejected by her friends. I read a diary entry that said, 'Now that I've begun to walk the talk, I've lost friends at school. But I will not hide the life God has put in me. If I have to sacrifice everything, I will. If my friends have to become enemies in order to keep my best Friend, Jesus, so be it.'"

Then, very softly, he said, "Rachel felt that God had showed her that she was going to reach her generation for Christ, but . . . she knew it had to be soon. She wrote that she didn't believe she would live long enough even to get married."

Scott looked at me with sad eyes, yet smiled. "Tonight brought a lot of that into focus for the first time. Thanks for a wonderful trip."

Watching him walk down the slope to his tent, I marveled that a nameless meadow on an obscure Iranian ridge could hold such rich meaning for a group of Americans. I walked up the meadow to the tent entrance, where David knelt, organizing his gear.

"Feel it?" he asked. "It's raining."

A soft, gentle rain had indeed begun to fall. But when we looked up, we saw nothing but stars.

"It must have blown in from some of those clouds over the summit," said Bright, listening from the shadows a few feet away. He had decided to sleep in the open and set his sleeping bag on the dewy grass so he could fall asleep watching the stars.

As we zipped up our tents, the campsite grew still. We listened to the soft, mournful wail of the Kangal pups whining in the shepherd's camp and heard the collar chains of the adult dogs jostling down by the fire pit. Then the night became quiet and peaceful.

Suddenly Bright's husky voice shattered the cool mountain quiet.

"I can't believe I'm in Iran!" he shouted. And with that I rolled over and fell asleep, scarcely believing it myself.

FINAL ASCENT

Our energy level had peaked. Well-fed and well-rested, we woke at first light, ate a quick breakfast of hot tea, flat bread, goat cheese, and yogurt, donned sweaters and gloves, and strapped on our packs. As I warmed my hands by the fire pit in the minutes before we left, my eyes drifted toward the patch of grass where yesterday's blood had spilled. It had disappeared. I remember thinking that the rain must have washed it away.

Dan Toth, more eager than any of us to see what lay over the ridge, broke out in front, endlessly checking his compass and GPS and occasionally swerving around to bark critiques of our climbing technique. It wasn't a tough climb, and we soon arrived at the big gorge that Dan said held the ark. I saw him staring intently into the ravine. It was much smaller than even Dan had expected. Instead of the yawning gorge we knew as Davis Canyon, we saw a deep, rolling meadow, hollowed out like a bowl beneath an arching rim of granite-laced foothills.

I looked at Dan and asked, "Where's the deep, ugly gorge you've been telling us about?" He didn't answer—he just kept staring down at the basin.

All of us began to scan the valley floor, but where we should have seen an ark, we saw a patchwork of mossy, snow-fed meadows, rugged moraine fields, and—surprisingly—a number of large, rectangular corrals built by the local shepherds to partition their flocks. These rugged corrals were hand-built out of loose, jagged rock, each piece looking ready to topple but fitting together like bricks in a wall. We had seen them scattered throughout the hills, as common as the domed tents on the outskirts of every shepherd's camp. But seeing them from this perspective—in this light and from this distance—they appeared oddly . . . *ark* shaped. Though each looked far too small to be the huge, rectangular outline we had seen in the satellite image, they were additional evidence (if any more were needed) that our target site amounted to little more than a well-traveled pasture, *anything* but remote and inaccessible. We could see man's fingerprints everywhere. On the far side of the basin, a shepherd tended his flock; Kangal dogs prowled a nearby meadow.

Dan remained quiet and aloof, staring at his charts, his eyes flitting up and down, endlessly scanning the basin and trying to align every facet, feature, and landmark that now seemed to have vanished. What had looked so compelling on the maps and in satellite comparisons with Davis's sketch at ground level appeared as little more than random wrinkles, folds, and outcroppings carved by wind, rain, and winter runoff. The huge rectangle that Dan incessantly assured me had to be the ark wasn't there. Its subtle lines had either dissolved into the elements or looked so different at ground level that we couldn't distinguish it from other rubble. The satellite image, Dan reminded me, was taken more than ten years ago.

"Whatever that shape was might simply have washed away during runoff," he said, "or been buried by rock slides. There was an earthquake up here a few years back, so anything's possible."

Hearing those words now struck a bitter chord. He was telling me that the hazy outline could have been *anything*.

"Show me the object, Dan," I said, trying to modulate my voice. But his eyes seemed frozen, glaring dumbstruck at his chart. He brushed me off and could now only stand there dismayed by it all.

"Just a *minute*," he said, followed by several tense moments of silence. "I don't know . . . this doesn't make sense." Finally, after another long interval of silence, he muttered, "It's *got* to be here."

I had observed it many times before in my many ark searches. With Dan huddled over the map murmuring to himself, it was evident that he had that old familiar malady. Even though he was trained as a Navy SEAL, he had one of the worst cases of ark fever I had ever seen.

Later that morning, our Land Rovers pulled out of camp. There would be no ark on this trip, and I was beginning to think that it would never be found. The mountains around me were vast—almost six hundred square miles of peaks and valleys, canyons and hills. I turned and looked once more at the crest of Mount Sabalon, its frigid peak obscured under a thick mantle of haze.

PART 7
Another Trip to Mount Ararat

CHAPTER 18

THE MCGIVERN VENTURE

Colorado Springs, April 2004

Over the next three years, I purchased an assortment of satellite photos of Mount Sabalon's general region and sent them to Dr. Holroyd for further analysis. I still thought that Mount Sabalon might be the mountain where Ed Davis saw his object during World War II, and I hoped that Dr. Holroyd would be able to see something of it on the satellite images—anything that might help us narrow down our search.

After diligently poring over the images of Mount Sabalon, the professor concluded that there was nothing resembling an ark-shaped object on the mountain. He commended Dan Toth's efforts, but told me regretfully that Dan's analysis of the satellite imagery had been wrong. Further arduous study by Dr. Holroyd showed no other terrain on Sabalon that remotely compared with Ed Davis's testimony. Mount Sabalon seemed to be sitting in the right geographical region to suggest it might have been Noah's final port, but in the end, nothing was there.

Hearing Dr. Holroyd's conclusion was disheartening. I had held onto a glimmer of hope, but now I knew it was time to give up on Mount Sabalon. I made a mental list of my progress to date. After almost twenty years of laborious research by land, horse, plane, helicopter, and satellite imagery, all I had ever found were natural formations of rock or ice, or empty canyons of lost dreams. Maybe it was time to treat my own case of ark fever by forgetting the whole ordeal. But one thing still beckoned me—I could not escape Ed Davis's story.

Maybe old Ed hadn't seen the ark at all but merely saw something that he *believed* was the ancient ship. I was sitting right there when he took the lie detector test and passed it without a hitch. I was there when he described seeing beams of a big wooden ship high on an unknown mountain in that amazing summer of 1943. I knew Ed Davis personally, and I believed him. I couldn't conjure up a single reason to doubt his veracity as a witness. Of all the sensational claims by people who claimed they'd seen the ark, Ed Davis's testimony still remained the most captivating.

DRAWN BACK IN

On April 27, 2004, a man named Dan McGivern held a news conference at the National Press Club in Washington, D.C., to announce that he was 98 percent certain he had identified the location of Noah's ark high on the slopes of Mount Ararat. McGivern had seen an unusual satellite image of the Turkish mountain, and he and several others were convinced that a dark object sticking out of the Abich II Glacier was man-made, and possibly the surviving hull of Noah's old boat.

The story raced around the world, but I held no such optimism. After all, I have heard many such claims over the past twenty years, and I suspected that this would be yet another disappointment for ark searchers.

I did have to admit, however, that this particular sighting was more intriguing than most because the satellite photos were taken during Europe's hottest summer in five hundred years. The scorching weather was so severe that it resulted in more than 20,000 deaths. It was no surprise to learn that the ice cap on Mount Ararat had experienced a drastic meltback, probably the greatest of our lifetime. The McGivern team announced that the ark was clearly exposed and that they planned to send several teams of scientists and cameramen (as many as thirty men) to investigate Ararat's slopes and record the historic findings.

Several months passed, and I heard through the grapevine that the planned McGivern expedition was stalled because the Turkish government was withholding permission to climb Mount Ararat. I also heard that more than two hundred teams had applied to climb the mountain, but I had no way of verifying those statistics. I'm sure that the numbers were quite high because of the overwhelming publicity surrounding the satellite images. Several teams of reporters flocked to the mountain like hungry birds of prey, but when nothing happened, they eventually packed up and moved on.

One day that summer, I received a phone call from a woman named Deborah, who introduced herself as Dan McGivern's daughter. She said that her father was frustrated with the bureaucratic red tape of trying to get to Mount Ararat. Deborah was one of the most sincere and kind people I have ever spoken with, and she was distressed by her father's poor treatment by the Turkish authorities. She had recently read a book of mine and felt that I had the experience to get things on track. I had been treated harshly by the Turks myself and knew all too well the snarl of bureaucracy over anything to do with the Ararat region. Deborah asked if I would go to Hawaii to meet her father and see if I could help in any way. It happened that I had an upcoming two-week speaking tour in New Zealand, and I decided to extend my return layover in Honolulu to meet her dad.

Dan McGivern picked me up at my hotel in Honolulu and drove me up the winding road to his house, perched high on a hill above the pounding surf of Oahu's windward coast. Dan and his wife, Melly, were wonderful hosts and eagerly showed me the satellite images of the object he hoped was the ark. Carefully scanning the images, I felt that they were interesting but far from convincing. After our meeting, Dan drove me back to the airport so I could catch my homeward flight.

"Bob, would you consider helping in the search?" Dan asked.

"I think it's too late for me to come in," I answered. "You already have an expedition leader and team selected. I'll be happy to give whatever advice I can."

"The Turks have yet to grant climbing permits for my team, and I don't know why."

I knew why. "Your team is too large. Requesting permits for a team of thirty looks suspicious to the Turks. They'll never grant permission to a thirty-person team. To them, that's a security risk."

"A security risk?"

"Exactly. Heavily armed Kurdish terrorists are holed up in caves on the mountain, and there is a long-standing bitter rift between the Kurds and the Turkish government. But they don't want the world to know that. If the world were exposed to the fact that a civil war was raging there, it would cause political embarrassment to a government that has worked very hard to enter the European Union and gain the Western world's acceptance."

"I should send a smaller team, then," Dan said.

"That's my suggestion. Send a two-man climb team that has experience with the treacherous terrain. A small team supported by a few Kurds will have the advantage of stealth. Once you've seen what is there, then you can tell the world what you've found, but until then, no more publicity."

He listened to my advice and graciously wished me well as he left me at the airport. Aside from a few more courtesy calls between us, I felt that the matter was over and my input was no longer needed. That is, until his daughter called. Deborah hinted that her dad could still use some assistance.

"What would you do, Bob?" she asked.

Without much consideration of the implications, I answered, "There's a good chance that I could get to the object, but it would be risky and probably too expensive."

She apparently took my suggestion (or boast) as some kind of commitment and was delighted that I would help. She said she was going to call her father right away, and before I knew it, she had hung up the phone.

I stood there in silence, looking out the window, thinking, *What a crazy thing to say. What was I thinking? I can get to the object? Was I subtly hoping for an invitation to become involved?*

I didn't believe that McGivern's object was even on the right mountain. But with the autumn years of life fast approaching and my youth fading dimly in the rearview mirror, did I still need to prove something? I had already made it up to the Ahora Gorge. I had navigated past the terrorists and the military patrols, and I had even climbed the mountain blind, at night. I didn't need to prove a thing. I'd had the worst experience of my life on the slopes of Ararat. I had almost died on that mountain, and now I was flirting with the prospect of doing it again?

I soon learned that the Turkish government had denied Dan McGivern's request for his team's climbing permit, along with all other applications that year. McGivern called me and—as I suspected he would—asked if I would get to his object. I wished that I hadn't bragged to Deborah that I thought I could.

I didn't know of a good reason other than ego for doing this trip. I knew that this was the most publicized sighting in history of an object thought to be Noah's ark, and I knew it would make good material for my book on the subject. And with Mount Ararat experiencing its greatest meltback in recorded history, conditions were as advantageous as they would ever be. Add to that some of the finest-quality satellite reconnaissance images, and if ever there was a time to find the ark—or to prove that it wasn't there—this was the year.

Dan McGivern had spent well over $100,000 on the project so far, and it held little prospect of success without some sort of boost. I told him that it would be pricey to mount an expedition with so little time to prepare, but he didn't hesitate and asked what I needed to get the job done. He offered me the biggest payday of my life if I could somehow find a way to get to the object and photograph it.

We both knew that it was late in the season and that the snows could come at any time, so speed was essential. I called my old climbing partner, Bob Stuplich, and after I told him how much he would be compensated for a successful mission, he agreed to go.

I then asked Jon Arnold, my former police academy classmate and now a retired captain from the Huntington Beach Police Department, to head the safety team. Jon and another friend, Kim Orr, would carry a satellite phone to call the U.S. embassy in Turkey if we met with any big problems while climbing. If we came to grief on the mountain, they were to notify our next of kin.

That left one more hurdle: my wife, Terry.

She wasn't buying "I want to change paradigms on the ark's location" or "It will make the book more exciting." She wasn't even persuaded by how much McGivern would pay for my services.

"No," she said with arms folded. "You are over fifty years old, and the only reason you want to do it is because the younger guys can't."

Busted! I cast my eyes down. She was right. I was intrigued by the promise of a big payday, but the thrill of setting out on another adventure, of tasting the cold wind in my teeth one more time, was really what was drawing me back. I wanted to stand at 17,000 feet and know that so many others wanted to get there but couldn't. I wanted to do it for all the nonsensical, irrational, male reasons that women prefer not to understand.

I looked into Terry's almond eyes, dredging my simple mind for some logical explanation that would gain her support. She has seen me leave to film the war in Afghanistan and head off to countless other hostile situations. She is so beautiful and kind, yet she possesses a strength I will never have. Knowing that I really wanted to give it a try, she forced a smile, slid her arms around my neck, and nuzzled her face next to mine.

"I'll keep the life insurance agent on speed dial," she whispered.

After I told Dan McGivern I would do it, I felt awkward about my new mercenary role. For the first time, I would be climbing without the spiritual mission that had seen me through the rigors of so many other expeditions. I was certain that our destination this time was only a big black hunk of rock that maybe looked like an ark. I wasn't driven by ark fever, only by the promise of an ample payday for photographing a mysterious object high on a mountain that was crawling with dangers.

Understanding fully the magnitude of what we were about to do, I set about planning the expedition.

DIVING FOR COVER

I pulled my rifle close to my chest and dove headfirst into a nest of leaves beside a rotting log, making myself as small a target as possible. I curled into a ball and lay still. The cries of my advancing foes echoed from the gully as my heart thumped and sweat trickled down my forehead.

I considered my next move. There were only three more hours of daylight on this late summer day, but the narrow ravine, sheltered by a thick canopy of tree branches, was already shaded. Twelve men scurried up the ridge to my left. I was not in a good position if they flanked me; they could easily pick me off. There was only one chance—to run through the thicket of trees just to my right and hope for the best.

A man shot at me from above, and chunks of tree bark sprayed my face.

"I got him! I got him!" my attacker shouted.

Unable to wait another second, I stood and ran up the hill. A stinging sensation nipped my left shoulder, and pain seared my right calf. I was hit! I dropped to the ground like a shot deer and lay there, stunned and hurt, as shots peppered the ground all around me. Instinctively, I stood up, but my injured leg failed me, and I fell again. Pulling myself across the loamy soil, I crawled behind a nearby elm tree and knew it was all over. I had to give up.

As I raised my rifle in surrender, my good friend David Halbrook saw me lying on the ground and ran to help me. He hoisted me up, and I limped up the ridge out of sight of the screaming gunmen and their relentless barrage.

"What a blast!" David said as we stopped, out of breath. "That was the most fun I have had all year!"

His exuberance soon dissolved as I removed my clear-plastic face shield and winced in agony.

"You all right?" he asked. I carefully lowered myself to the ground, and David noticed the lime-green paint oozing down my right sleeve.

I had been in a battle, but fortunately I wasn't fighting for my life. It was a paintball game at a men's retreat where I was the weekend speaker for a church in the Shenandoah Valley of Virginia. I looked down at my calf, expecting to see a splotch of paint to correspond with the searing pain in my leg, but there wasn't a mark there. Instead, it turned out, I had torn my calf muscle running up the hill. As I tried to stand on my own, I wished I hadn't agreed to play in the late afternoon game. The next day, I was scheduled to fly to Turkey, where I would lead a climbing team up 17,000-foot Mount Ararat in search of Dan McGivern's object. What was I going to do? I tried walking, but I couldn't take even the smallest steps.

The next morning, things weren't much better. The ripped muscle was painful, and I could barely walk. What I really needed was a pair of crutches. After breakfast, David Halbrook called every pharmacy in the area before he drove me out to Dulles Airport, but he was unable to locate any crutches. I had no choice but to tough it out. When my three-man team met me at the gate for our flight, they thought I was joking until they saw the pain on my face with every step I took.

It was a bad way to start an expedition.

CHAPTER 19

WHATEVER CAN GO WRONG . . .

Turkey, September 2004

After stops in Istanbul and Ankara, we arrived in Erzurum. From there, we took a four-hour cab ride to the mountain. Now came the tricky part. I had no idea how I would get permission to climb from the Turkish military and the Kurdish PKK freedom fighters. Then I still had to get to the object on the mountain. This late in the season, unexpected snow could cut loose when we were high on the mountain, trapping the team in such deep snow that we could never get down. Avalanches and falling boulders were always a problem, and without the right permissions, we could be shot by the Turkish military at the lower elevations or the Kurdish gueril-las on the higher regions of the mountain. The full realization of those potential scenarios smacked me in the face as the huge beast of a mountain called Ararat came into full view. I had forgotten just how large the mountain was.

We drove to the small village of Dogubayazit at the base of Ararat, looking for Micah, our previous guide who had made all of the arrangements for Dick Bright. We found bad news. Micah's father told us that his son was in jail for killing a Turkish man in a family dispute. With Micah paying his debt to Turkish society, it was time for our backup plan.

Unfortunately, we had no backup plan.

Sitting at an outdoor restaurant, I tried to keep a game face for my team. I was talking the situation over with Bob Stuplich when a man introduced himself to us as Micah's brother Si. He was a well-dressed Kurd of about thirty, with short, coarse black hair the same color as his penetrating dark eyes. Si scooted up a chair and sat down, telling us that he had recently been on the mountain and had found over twenty skeletons of Kurds, their bones bleaching in the glaring sun as their rusted rifles lay by their sides.

"The Turks are very hard to deal with because of all the fighting these days," he said. Then, with a crooked smile, he commented, "I assume you are here to climb the mountain. I can help."

In short order, we asked if he could get us to an object that we wanted to photograph on the Abich II Glacier. Si told us that he had many contacts in the military and that perhaps he could make a deal with them for safe transport up the mountain.

"But," he added, "it will be very expensive." He clasped his hands behind his head as if to say, "You guys have no other choice but to use my services."

He was right, and as he leaned back in his chair waiting for my response, I saw the glint of chrome from a 9 mm pistol stuck in his waistband.

In a nutshell, the situation was that 11,000 Turkish troops stationed around the lower elevations of the mountain were trying to control about 2,000 PKK terrorists higher on the mountain. The factions were locked in brutal civil war, and we were supposed to pay off both the Turkish military and the Kurdish guerillas just to let us walk through their ongoing hostilities. We had to climb a monster mountain with ominous perils of its own, and we had to get to McGivern's object.

The only way to do all this seemed to be in the hands of a shifty, unproven character I had just met, who was negotiating his services by flashing a handgun in front of me. I didn't like the feel of it, but I was not there for my feelings. Stuplich and I both knew there was a very big payday waiting if we could get the job done.

By now, the romantic lure of ego and adventure had long since faded away. I contemplated the shifting dynamics of my predicament. I had more than $30,000 taped under the insoles of my shoes in $100 bills, and stood at least an inch taller. Any payment to military or PKK fighters on the mountain would be no problem. My big worry was that Si would shoot me if he knew I had so much cash.

Si invited me to his home for dinner to continue the negotiations. When I arrived, he instructed me to take off my shoes and leave them on the front steps. His house fronted a narrow street where villagers were milling about. It is a Muslim tradition to remove shoes before entering a home, and I had no choice but to take them off and place them upside down on his front porch. After dinner, I was relieved when I found the shoes with all their concealed cash still inside.

Our plan was soon set. I agreed to the steep fees imposed by Si for climbing approval and was trying to be as hopeful as possible that my leg would get better in time to climb. The plan was simple: get up fast, get to the object, take a photo of whatever it was, and get off the mountain. It was a seemingly uncluttered plan, but there were a million things that could go wrong.

We stayed in a small cement hovel at the edge of town to avoid being noticed by the locals—police or military. Two days later, at 4:00 AM, Si kicked at our door and said, "We go."

A Russian-made jeep-like contraption rolled up in the dark, and we stacked our packs on top. Stuplich, Kim, Jon, Si, a Kurdish climber named Juma, and I jammed ourselves inside a space made for no more than four men. We drove around the west side of the mountain on a paved highway that eventually turned toward Ahora village on Ararat's north slope. There we bounced along on a narrow dirt road that wound its way up the lower slopes where three men armed with Kalashnikov machine guns met us. It was now early daylight. The men asked a few questions of Si, who glanced over at us and explained the situation.

The men waved us past with no problem. Si turned to me with unabashed arrogance, saying, "Those were Turkish military men, we are free to go up."

It appeared that our sizable payment of passage was working for now, but we still had the Kurdish PKK to worry about higher on the mountain.

The squatty little vehicle struggled up the rutted path, mile after jarring mile, heading for the higher elevations. Fields of wheat, endless stacked rock walls, and children herding sheep and cattle surrounded us. The children were young, barely able to lift the big sticks they used to whack the bony rumps of cows and prod stub-born sheep along.

We continued to climb. Small clusters of black wool nomad tents dotted the rolling hills, framed by sharply cut bluffs. Kurdish women carried large plastic water jugs lashed to their backs, their brightly colored dresses and flowing scarves billowing in the cool mountain breeze. Men with bushy black mustaches on their leath-ery faces watched as we drove past, but did nothing.

Several huge dogs ferociously attacked our vehicle's tires. One hairy beast even bit at the threadbare rubber. Immediately, we heard the sickening sound of his skull slamming against the wheel well. Turning back, we watched the dog cartwheel in the dust, roll to a stop, and then spring to its feet to run after us again.

At about 8,000 feet, we came to a nomad village on the side of a valley. Five wool tents framed a large flock of sheep. Several young children stopped their play and scampered over to greet us. Smoke swirled around an open fire tended by Kurdish women who quickly covered their faces with their multi-colored cotton scarves.

"We stay here," Si said, unlatching the creaking door of the jeep and stepping out onto the hard ground. A stocky, unshaven Kurd of about forty-five, the elder of the camp, strode over and hugged Si. "These are friends," Si said. "We will be safe in his camp."

That was comforting, because I knew we were right in the mid-dle of terrorist country. As I got out of the crammed jeep and stretched, I couldn't help noticing a peg-legged young man stand-ing in the distance. He stared at us, standing with a wild-looking, dirty man who clutched a beat-up shotgun. The pair never took their eyes off us as we unloaded our gear.

"Who are they?" I asked.

Si whispered, "The man with one leg is a rebel fighter with the PKK. His leg was recently cut off because of a bullet wound he received from a Turkish soldier. The other is famous."

"Famous? How?"

"He has killed twenty-four people. They call him the 'Young Assassin.'"

"Charming," I said.

My sarcasm was wasted on Si. "The Turkish government pays poor Kurds who live below the mountain to be village guards. They provide information against the PKK guerillas, but anyone who helps the Turks is targeted for death by the Young Assassin. He slips into their homes at night and slits their throats while they sleep. He then stuffs money in their mouths as a warning for others not to provide information against the PKK."

The assassin glanced at me, his vacant black eyes mirroring his dark soul. He knew that Si was talking about him, and he smiled at me with nicotine-stained teeth, cradling his shotgun.

Si's cell phone chirped from his pocket. After a loud and animated conversation, he hung up and explained that a Kurdish official higher on the mountain had instructed that only one member of our group would be allowed to climb up. He would have to go with one Kurdish climber and be escorted partway up the mountain by the Young Assassin. The caller also demanded that we take a prescribed route up the mountain because the PKK was operating out of a nearby cave.

Without hesitating, Stuplich said he would be the one to head up with the two Kurds. Si told me that Juma would go with Stuplich and the Young Assassin. It was a hastily arranged plan, and after another round of animated discussions between the Kurds, it was set.

I had no choice but to go along with this, but I didn't like being left behind. The fact was that I probably couldn't have gotten all the way up the mountain with my bad leg. If all went well, Bob would locate the object the next afternoon and be snapping away with his digital camera at whatever it turned out to be. They were packed in ten minutes, and with game smiles, Stuplich and the two Kurds headed up.

After the climbers left, a young boy from the nomad's village brought us each a steaming cup of tea. Si took a sip of the sweet brew and lowered himself onto a big rock as he rubbed his stubbled face.

"Six days ago," he said, "three Russians went up the same route as your friend and the two Kurds. The Russians did not pay the PKK as we have done, and because of that, they were killed, shot in the head. It was a most unfortunate thing to have happen. I need to renegotiate some extra pay to avoid an unfortunate accident from happening to Bob."

"And how much will that cost?" I asked, knowing I was dealing with a pirate who had maneuvered me to the end of the gangplank.

As if his words were carried on the winds of absolute sincerity, he told me, "Any additional fees will be minimal—to be discussed later, of course." Most Kurds in these parts are going to try their best to get all you have in your wallet, but my main concern was for my friend who was hiking somewhere in the swirling clouds above. Waiting it out in camp with Kim Orr, Jon Arnold, and Si was all I could do for now.

We set up camp and prayed that night for Stuplich and Juma to make it up and down the mountain alive. A majestic orange sun greeted us in the morning, and news from Stuplich via Juma's cell phone reported tough going. The Young Assassin had retreated at about the 10,000-foot level the night before, leaving Stuplich and Juma on their own to make it to the ice cap. Stuplich told Si that loose rock scree and sheer cliffs had stalled their efforts and they might not be able to go any further. Massive rocks were crashing around them—to traverse these treacherous boulder fields, Stuplich and Juma had to time the rate of the falling rocks, then scurry across the mountainside before another loose boulder came hurtling down on them.

"There were so many rocks falling," Stuplich would later say, "that it was difficult to see how the mountain would be more than a nub a hundred years from now."

It was treacherous climbing, and Stuplich became angry that Si had sent them up such a difficult route. At 10:00 AM, Si got another call on his cell phone from Juma, who had twisted his knee when his boot slid off a rock. Stuplich later described Juma as "writhing in pain" from the injury.

Si hung up and with a concerned expression said, "We have to go find Juma. Bob cannot carry Juma's seventy-pound pack down with his own and help Juma. Juma says he will not leave his pack up there."

Stuplich told Juma he was going to head down and drop off his heavy load and return to get him because he was the only one who could find Juma again. I thought it a poor plan because it would be too exhausting for Stuplich. I remember his telling me many times that you never leave someone alone on the mountain. Perhaps he thought that Juma was experienced and had enough food, water, and warm clothes to make it for the time being. I tried to talk to Stuplich on the phone to convince him to stay put because we would climb up and help them, but we lost the connection and I couldn't reconnect.

I looked at my leg, which only six days earlier had been so bad that I was trying to buy crutches to walk to the plane. Now I was thinking of going up the lip of the Ahora Gorge to assist an injured climber. Kim couldn't go—he was beyond sick and lying in his tent after eating some unsanitary food. Jon Arnold had no mountain-climbing experience, so he wasn't an option. That left me.

We hurled our packs onto the jeep's luggage rack and drove up a wisp of dirt road, trying to squeeze in a little more altitude before heading up on foot. We made it about a mile to a twenty-tent no-mad camp bustling with people. Jon came with us to guard the jeep while we climbed.

We left the jeep, and I hurriedly shouldered my pack. I took a quick look at Jon, who stood alone with fifty Kurds gawking at him as if he were from Mars. Most nomads have never seen a West-erner. It was also strange for Jon because he had never traveled overseas before. It was a slight moment of levity, but I soon lost my smile as I glanced up at the big mountain, crowned with ice and shrouded in afternoon clouds.

"What about the terrorists up there?" I asked Si.

He said nothing, which to me said a lot.

After half an hour of hiking, my leg began loosening up, and by using a ski pole as a cane, I could keep a slow but steady pace. We trekked a snaking ridgeline on the western edge of the enormous gorge. Boulders as large as automobiles hurtled down the slope, sending a guttural rumble through the ground and up my legs.

Misty clouds exhaled from the ancient, stained-black glaciers on the floor of the gorge, like steam rising from a two-mile-wide cauldron. Icy wind swirled off the summit to stir the angry clouds. When these clouds descended on us, it became impossible to see, but in an instant, a brilliant sun flashed in my eyes as they slipped past. Si kept a constant vigil, looking up at the ridgeline and eventually spotting a small figure. It was Juma, sitting in some boulders about a mile away. He was alone.

Later I learned that we had somehow crossed paths with Stuplich. He eventually hiked to a nomad camp, and after hearing from the locals that we had gone up for Juma, he crashed on the floor of the nomad tent and fell asleep.

When we got to Juma, Si hugged him and quickly hoisted his friend's big pack on his back. I assisted the injured climber all the way down, and when we made it to Jon and the jeep, Juma and I were limping in unison.

We rumbled back to camp in the jeep, where Stuplich immediately confronted Si, venting his frustration. Although Stuplich was very experienced on Ararat, he had never been up the northern route and was at the mercy of Juma, who was also unfamiliar with the dangerous route. There was no explanation from Si as to why he had sent Stuplich up such a perilous route with a guide who knew nothing of the way. It made no sense, and all we could get out of Si was a deflated, "I'm sorry."

Maybe it was because of the terrorists who didn't want us snooping around in their backyard, or maybe it was for some other reason, but Si wouldn't say.

When Si saw that Stuplich and I were angry, he must have thought that the remainder of his payment would pass him by like clouds on the mountain. I am sure he realized that he had better find a way for us to get to McGivern's object. Si suggested that we try again the next morning from the south side of the mountain. Two experienced Kurdish climbers with good horses could be arranged. "With some good weather it could be done," Si said.

The southern route would be a much longer hike, but the terrorists weren't as prevalent there and it was a course that Stuplich knew well. I looked at him and saw that he was spent. I asked him what he was thinking.

He paused for a moment to gather his thoughts and then, staring up at the mountain, said, "I'm fifty-six years old, and that mountain beat me today, but I won't let it beat me again." Then he flashed a look at Si as if to say, "Don't ever do that to me again."

At 4:20 the next morning, I was packed and ready to go. I was going to climb with Stuplich, and my adrenaline had kicked in. We had returned to our camp just outside Dogubayazit late the night before and tried to get a few hours' rest and resupply for another attempt on the mountain. The jeep would show up at any minute to take us to the waiting pack horses at Eli village. After that, we would push hard to make it to the object. I knew that the next two days would possibly be the most challenging of my life. My calf ached from yesterday's climb to get Juma, but I had made it then, and just possibly I could make it all the way up today.

As Stuplich and I walked outside in the cold morning air, we looked toward the mountain but could not see it in the darkness. As I tried to conceal my limp, my friend clamped his hand tight on my shoulder and asked, "Are you 100 percent?"

"I'm okay," I replied.

Stuplich gripped harder and said with more intensity, "Tell me, Bob, right here, right now. Are you 100 percent?"

"Almost," I admitted. "I'll be fine."

Bob Stuplich had seen me gut it out on mountains before, and I was surprised when he chided, "You will be more of a problem than a help to me. You're not going."

I started to protest, but I knew he was right. My injury could compromise the whole mission and Stuplich's safety. If my leg caused me problems at high altitudes, there was no telling how bad things could get. The object we were hunting was embedded over a sheer drop-off, and it would take real alpine skill just to get to it.

We reached Eli village as the sun spread across the Anatolian plain. The settlement was a rock-walled cluster of crude mud and rock dwellings on the lower flank of the southern side of the mountain. A young boy was saddling three well-fed, good-looking sorrel horses.

Looking at the peak, I could see clouds already forming. I worried that the snowfall might arrive in the next few hours, making real trouble for Stuplich and the Kurds. I glanced at Stuplich and saw a steeled expression. He had been high on Ararat's punishing slopes and had almost died there once because of a snowstorm, but I sensed that he was going to climb no matter what he faced. I had seen so many others who had ark fever push themselves beyond reason, but never Stuplich. He was a cool customer and possessed the climbing ability of a cat. He had been climbing Ararat for over thirty years, establishing his impressive mountaineering résumé by leading climbs for high-profile expeditions. He had often endured hardship and physical agony beyond description, but he had never been beat on the mountain the way he had the day before. I could only wonder what he was thinking.

Stuplich is hard as nails. He is starting to stoop a little and is graying, but the spreading wrinkles across his once youthful face could not betray the fiery determination in his heart that would propel him up the demanding slopes. This was probably his last time up, and I think he wanted to make it to the object on his own terms. It wasn't a sentimental moment. Like me, he just needed to jam his ice ax into the mountain's high glacier, stare into the throat of the mighty Ahora Gorge, and know that he had won.

The young boy packed the horses, cinched the load, and brought the animals to the climbers.

"Don't get caught in snow," I cautioned, as he hiked off with his Kurdish guides. I was talking like a nervous father who just has to offer some last-minute advice, but Stuplich simply turned back without comment and flashed me his patented reassuring grin.

Si and I spent the next two hours at the local military base, where I shelled out a lot more money. Then we returned to our concrete hovel at the edge of Dogubayazit and waited. The top of the mountain remained dark with menacing clouds throughout the day and into the night. I knew that it would be brutally cold and miserable up there, but I remember thinking that this was probably the way Stuplich wanted it.

As I heard the story later, they made it to 12,000 feet by late afternoon and tied off the horses. Grass doesn't grow any higher on the mountain, so they left the animals to graze through the night. The horses would probably be in the most danger. Wolves prowl the slopes of Ararat and have attacked helpless horses before. Si told me that on his last trip up the mountain, wolves killed one of the packhorses during the night while he slept nearby. In chilling words, he described how he found the remains in the morning after the wolves had eaten its entrails and chewed off its snout. It was a mental picture I could have done without.

After leaving the horses, they went on to 14,000 feet and stopped for a short sleep. At 2:00 AM, they rose and advanced toward the ice. It was a bitter cold morning, inky black with a cutting wind. Stuplich had a camel water container, a plastic bladder with a drinking tube strapped over the shoulder. The water in the camel froze solid, and to make the situation worse, someone at the nomad village had stolen his gloves the previous day, which Stuplich didn't realize until he was high on the mountain. This could be a real problem in such frigid conditions. The block of ice on his back made Stuplich shiver, but he knew he needed body heat to thaw out enough water to drink.

After an hour or so, they stopped for a snack of goat butter and bread, but the stop made the cold seem worse, so they resumed walking. At 7:00 AM, they finally made the 16,444-foot saddle that was beyond the early morning shadows and into the warming sun. Stuplich increased the pace but the Kurds couldn't keep up—they were suffering from cerebral edema from the fast ascent and had debilitating headaches. When he came upon the first deep ice crevasses that stretched across the huge glaciers, the Kurds stopped in protest. Apparently they did not have the confidence to walk over the crevasses, which were three to five feet wide. Ice crevasses are very long openings in the ice that drop down as much as one hundred feet into the bowels of the glacier.

The only way to cross is to walk across snow bridges, which are little more than drifting snow piles over a crevice that melt in the afternoon sun and freeze at night. The process creates a crusted ice platform, but the brittle snow bridges are often unstable and very unpredictable, so climbers rope themselves together. In theory, if one fell through, the other two could pull the fallen comrade out.

At this point, the Kurds refused to go any further. Stuplich thought the snow bridges looked good, but they can give way at any time even when they look passable. Stuplich understood the dangers. If he went in alone and fell, he would be wedged like a human cork in a grave of eternal ice.

With spiked crampons on his feet and carrying a metal ice ax in each of his bare hands, Stuplich went on without the Kurds, who sat down on the big glacier and shouted, "Crazy man," as he disappeared over the vast ridge. When Stuplich finally made it to the gorge, he peered into the rocky abyss.

I can remember the first time I saw that gorge five years earlier. My knees went limp and my heart crawled up my throat. Stuplich was going to walk alone down its sixty-degree ice slope to the object. If he slipped, he would hurtle over the lip of the gorge and freefall for 4,000 feet before coming to a very abrupt stop on a slab of rock.

Stuplich was 150 feet above the object, and he could not climb down the steep wall of ice any further. He had pushed the boundary of extreme controlled risk and was now in the realm of insanity. He twisted a five-inch ice screw deep into the ice. Then he strung a nylon rope through the carabiner on his waist harness and attached it to the ice screw. He grabbed the frozen 150-foot rope with bare hands and lowered himself inch by inch. Massive clumps of clouds started to crawl out of the gorge. Rocks were avalanching below him, and the wind seared his bare hands as he gripped the icy rope. In a few minutes, he was finally there, standing on Dan's ark object.

He was not surprised to find that it was made of rock and ice.

After taking many pictures of the place to verify that he was actually on the right object, he shifted his thoughts to getting up and out. Looking around one last time at the awesome grandeur of the mountain, he stood still and took in the moment. This mountain was all his now. He could feel his heart moving in rapid thumps and heard his lungs laboring to suck in the thin, cold air.

The dark clouds mushroomed around him. Within the hour, it would start snowing, so he had to hurry. He pulled himself up the frozen rope with the cold numbing his hands. When he got to the top, he was exhausted. He considered taking time to unscrew the fifty-five dollar ice screw he had set in the glacier, but didn't. After he trekked back across the big glacier, he and the Kurds hiked off the ice cap. Once they made it onto rocky terrain, the snows let loose, descending in sleeting waves. The trio set a blistering pace and made it down to Eli village by nightfall.

It was one of the most daring, courageous, and perhaps insane feats I know of, and Bob Stuplich did it. That night around dinner, a weary Stuplich said that it was the greatest experience of his life, and that he could now say good-bye to his old friend and nemesis, Mount Ararat.

Calling Dan McGivern at his home in Hawaii was a hard thing to do. He had paid us well to get the job done, and I deeply respected his motives for the search. Like so many others, he felt sure that he had seen the ghost ship of Noah and that this discovery would change the world and introduce the lost to God. We returned to the States, saying nothing to the press. McGivern told us, "I want no publicity for now."

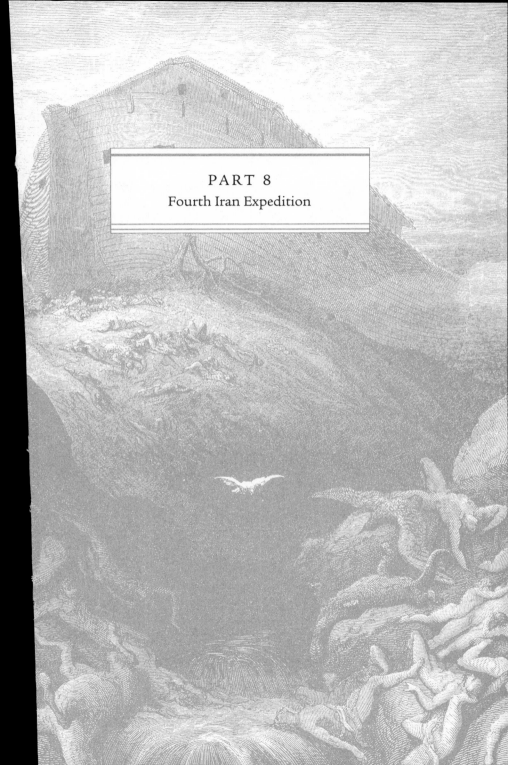

PART 8
Fourth Iran Expedition

CHAPTER 20

ONE LAST TRY

Colorado Springs, November 2004

After twenty years of searching for Ed Davis's mountain, I was tired of the hunt. I was weary of the cold climbs, the draining expenses, the disappointment, and the ridicule. As my ark fever rapidly succumbed to reason, I found myself putting my maps and climbing gear in my storage closet, closing the door on my lost dreams. At long last, I was saying good-bye to old Noah.

But Dr. Ed Holroyd wasn't quite finished with the Ed Davis story. As an adjunct professor at the University of Denver, Dr. Holroyd teaches courses about remote sensing and image processing, in addition to his role as a remote-sensing scientist for the U.S. Bureau of Reclamation. He has the necessary expertise to analyze and evaluate satellite reconnaissance imagery. Over the past couple of years, he had taken it upon himself to analyze Ed Davis's testimony one last time.

Dr. Holroyd compiled scraps of evidence from the Ed Davis story and sifted through the fragmented pieces, following Davis's route from Hamadan, where Badi's family had taken the young sergeant in July 1943. He looked at the archives of Davis's interviews and meticulously scanned the maps that Davis himself had helped to sketch. One map in particular was drawn by renowned artist Elfred Lee. Relying on Ed Davis's expertise as an engineer, the pair had drafted a sketch of the terrain as Davis remembered it. Though it is doubtful that anyone could recall every minute detail after so many years, Davis was able to describe peaks, directions of water flow, snow fields, and more. Lee also painted a beautiful panoramic scene of what Davis said he had seen. Using Davis's testimony, the maps and sketches by Elfred Lee, and an array of satellite images, Dr. Holroyd found what he firmly believed was a match to the gorge on a mountain in Iran where Ed Davis had said he'd been.

Davis had gone to the mountain with his Muslim guides but had never heard the name of the peak. He could recall travel times, going through Qazvin, and coming to a small village soon thereafter. He had started up the mountain on horseback, and then continued on foot when the terrain became too steep. It took him and his guides three days to reach the object.[†] It rained or snowed

---

[†] Over the years, several people have asked me why Ed Davis's Iranian driver, Badi Abas, and his family would go to such great lengths to take Ed up to the mountain where they believed the ark was. With all the rain, snow, and difficult climbing conditions, it doesn't seem to make a lot of sense. However, at the time that Ed Davis took the lie detector test in 1988, he gave me some background information that he didn't want disclosed until after he died. As an army sergeant stationed in Iran during World War II, he had taken some dynamite without the permission of his superiors and had given it to his driver, Badi Abas, for use in Badi's village. Badi had told him about a stream that used to flow through the village, providing water to the community, but which had been diverted by a rock slide in the area. The

almost the whole time, so he spent evenings in a series of caves. At one point as he went up, the air smelled of rotten eggs. He recalled certain geological features, such as a prominent peak called Doomsday Point, rock-slide areas, water flows, slopes, and the contours of a horseshoe-shaped valley. It was there that Davis saw what he described as the ark.

It was a nebulous set of clues, but Davis's engineering recollections were like a hurtling arrow to a target for Dr. Holroyd. As he cross-compared various satellite images with Davis's maps and his detailed descriptions, a road map emerged that led the way to a 15,300-foot peak on the southern rim of the Caspian Sea called Takht-e-Soleiman, "The Throne of Solomon."

After Dr. Holroyd completed his new research, he called me and announced, "I found it."

Here we go again, I thought. *Now ark fever has afflicted a university professor.*

The professor came to my office a few days after his surprising call and laid out several maps and satellite photos on my desk. I looked at them, but the stack of colored images from space and his lists of notes and mathematical calculations were too confusing for me. I asked Dr. Holroyd to explain. Methodically, he showed me how he had figured out where Ed Davis went on that momentous day more than sixty years ago.

---

dynamite was used to blow up the obstruction to allow water to flow freely through the village as it had before. Because Ed Davis solved this crucial problem, he was greatly esteemed by the village elders, including Badi's grandfather, Abas Abas. Through Badi, the elder Abas told Ed Davis that he wanted to repay him for his kindness, as was customary in the Iranian culture. Ed replied that the only thing he wanted in return was to see the remains of Noah's ark, which Badi had told him rested high in the mountains above the village. It was out of gratitude for what Ed Davis had done that the Abas family went to such extremes, in the face of such inclement weather, to assure that he would be granted his one request.

Ed Holroyd is a typical scholar. He measures his words, and his sharp eyes never stray from your face until he is sure you understand exactly what he is saying. By the time he finished his presentation, he had my full attention. Had I made a mistake in my previous research on Mount Sabalon? I had followed the words of Ed Davis and had tracked him from Hamadan to Qazvin and all the way to Mount Sabalon. But Dr. Holroyd had now come up with a different conclusion after a review of the mountains of northern Iran.

Dr. Holroyd had been involved in the Dan Toth expedition and was disappointed in his earlier analysis of the satellite photos. He had suggested that Toth's site had possibilities but admitted he hadn't given it a thorough review. I was a little cautious about trusting his assurances now, but he made a pretty good case for his new findings.

This time, he had doggedly examined every patch of mountain terrain in the entire search area. His conclusion was that we were all off the mark in thinking that Sabalon was the Davis mountain, and he was now confident he had finally found where Ed Davis had been.

I had initially thought that Davis went to Mount Sabalon, because it was the only mountain in the search area with a snowcap in July. Davis said that the peak of his mountain was visible 1,000 feet or so above where his ark object lay and that the object was embedded in deep snow. That would probably require a mountain more than 14,000 feet high.

When Larry Williams and I had come to a fork in the road on the way to Qazvin, we had looked at the maps and had taken the left fork, focusing on Mount Sabalon because of its height. It had honestly never occurred to me that Davis could have gone to the right at Qazvin, but I learned from Dr. Holroyd that to the right there are foothills that introduce a mountain range known as Solomon's Massif, located in the Mazandaran Province of northern Iran. This area borders the southern part of the Caspian Sea and includes several mountains over 15,000 feet (eighteen peaks are over 14,000 feet). Now, after looking at Dr. Holroyd's research, I considered that Davis's mountain could be one of them.

A third-century historian named Julius Africanus seems to agree that the ark might be in that area. He writes, "The Ark settled on the Mountains of Ararat, which we know to be in Parthia."[1] Parthia was a powerful ancient kingdom that ruled from the second century BC to the third century AD. It had a wide area of influence, and its borders expanded, contracted, and migrated over time. Interestingly, nineteenth-century mapmakers placed Parthia in northern Iran, just below the southern shores of the Caspian Sea, in the area of the Elburz Mountains—right where Dr. Holroyd suggested that Ed Davis had been.

Another interesting corroboration to the Ed Davis testimony is that this area is often drenched in rain and snow, receiving more than fifty-six inches of precipitation a year (as opposed to only nine inches in Tehran and a scant two inches farther south). This is an important clue because Ed Davis said he was rained on almost the entire time he traveled up and down the mountain. Nowhere else in Iran does the rain continue for such long durations in the summer months as it does along the southern shore of the Caspian Sea.

CHECKING WITH MY IRANIAN SOURCES

I contacted an Iranian mountaineering guide company by e-mail and asked about the Mazandaran region. I was surprised to receive the following e-mail on December 4, 2004:

> . . . Meanwhile, I should say that I have talked to a guide who is completely knowledgeable and aware of the region. [I] asked him the reason for calling this mountain range [Throne of Solomon] and he cited that he himself had seen a large piece of wood on the peak which unfortunately climbers and Shepard's [sic] had burned as fuel, but some remaining of it still can be found there.

I sent another e-mail to the mountain guide company and inquired about the apparent age of the wood. On December 26, 2004, I received the following reply:

> About the existing date of the wooden boards, no exact date is yet indicated. But as far as the elders of the region recalls [sic], the wooden boards had been there from the time when the first person had climbed the mountain and witnessed the boards.

Old wood on the very mountain identified by Dr. Holroyd!

The Iranians also described the mystery wood as being hand-hewn with an ax-type tool. My first response was, "Maybe old Ed Davis will soon be vindicated." I immediately ordered expensive high-resolution satellite images through Dr. Holroyd, with specific emphasis on the proposed Davis site. Unfortunately, Dr. Holroyd could not find an ark or any object even resembling the shape of an ark in these photos.

What in the world did Ed Davis see back then? He claimed conclusively that he saw actual boards from the ark, and a large, decomposing hull, but were those boards from an old altar site, a mine shaft, or some other construction? Wooden structures are not rare on mountains said to contain the ark. I know that an abundance of wood has been taken up Mount Ararat over the years, and perhaps the same is true of Mount Soleiman. According to Lloyd R. Bailey, in his book *Where Is Noah's Ark?*, Professor Friedrich Parrot hauled two crosses up Ararat's slopes, one five feet long and the other ten feet long. The larger one he erected at a 16,000-foot elevation and the smaller one he planted at the summit. A Russian colonel, J. Khodzko, also erected a seven-foot cross on the summit in 1859. In 1902, another party of Russians left a wooden container on the summit of Ararat. Two monasteries, each partially made of wood, were constructed at 6,350 feet and at 8,300 feet on Ararat's flanks.

If the local villagers considered Davis's mountain to be the holy site of Noah, then other such wooden shrines might have been built there as well. Did Davis see Noah's ark, or was he shown some wooden beams and left dreaming about what they might be? Based on Dr. Holroyd's new evidence, I knew that I had to go one last time to see what I could find.

As I began to plan yet another trip to Iran to look for the mountain of Noah among the soaring peaks of the Elburz range, I was reminded of an old Irish fisherman's prayer:

> Dear Lord, be good to me. The sea is so wide and my boat is so small.

CHAPTER 21

IS IT THE ARK—AT LAST?

Mount Soleiman, Iran, July 2005

I've heard it said that the eyes are windows to the soul. I can remember looking into Ed Davis's eyes just after he took his lie detector test, back in 1988, and feeling as if I were seeing straight into his vindicated soul. After so many years of people ridiculing his claim to have seen Noah's ark, he had passed the test. His integrity had been confirmed.

"I hope they now know that I was telling the truth," he whispered, leaning forward toward me in his chair.

I felt at the time, and I still feel it today, that I was sitting there with Ed Davis for a reason. On the strength of his testimony, I would venture repeatedly into distant, inhospitable places trying to find the object he had seen. And even though I always returned home with a backpack filled with disappointment, I never quite gave up hope that someday someone—and maybe it would be me—would find the exact spot where Ed Davis had stood.

Now, based on Dr. Ed Holroyd's convincing report that he had found Ed Davis's mountain and equipped with new satellite maps and a clear objective, I set off on July 5, 2005, for a one-week expedition to Mount Soleiman in northern Iran. At the time, this book was "basically done," in the words of my editor, but the publisher assured me that they would set aside a few pages at the end of the book for a last-minute report about my trip. None of us knew what we would find on the mountain—maybe it would be nothing—but I was hopeful that we would at least find the *place* where Ed Davis had seen whatever it was, and bring back some samples of the wood that reportedly had been found at high elevation on the mountain.

My team consisted of attorneys Doug Scherling and Steve Crampton, and Mike Morrison from Tyndale House Publishers. None of these guys—all family men, about my age, and serious about their faith in God—had a trace of ark fever, but they love adventure and had climbing experience, so I had invited them to come along. Steve and Doug are two of my closest friends, and I was happy when they agreed to go on my "farewell tour" looking for old Noah. I met Mike while attending a meeting at Tyndale House. He can best be described as a strong, quiet man with a gentle spirit. He grew up near the Rockies and is an accomplished climber. He would prove to be a valuable addition to the team.

JOURNEY TO "SOLOMON'S THRONE"

Arriving late at night in Tehran, we went immediately to our hotel to grab a few hours of sleep before heading to the imposing Elburz mountain range, which hugs the southern shores of the Caspian Sea.

Early the next morning, our Iranian tour guide, a man named Mohsen, greeted us in the hotel lobby. He was a thin young man, who walked with a limp, the result of a motorcycle accident that had mangled his leg. He later told us that, in the accident, he had been trapped under a car for six hours before the police arrived. When he was finally taken to the hospital, the doctors told him that the simple solution would be to lop off his injured foot. He declined that option and left the hospital with a severely damaged foot and a lifelong limp.

Mohsen was from the Qazvin area of Iran, the city that Ed Davis recalled passing through on his way to the mountain. I asked him about the large, gnarled grapevines that Ed Davis had reportedly seen near the base of the mountain, and he said, "Oh, yes, there are ancient vines in the area, and they are quite large, with big, twisted trunks."

After a six-hour drive, we arrived at the small town of Rudbarak, a picturesque, wooded hamlet at the base of an enormous mountain range. Its winding main street follows the contours of a robust, aqua blue river that filled the canyon walls with the constant sound of rushing water.

In Rudbarak, we met our climbing guide, Rasul, a fifty-four-year-old climbing machine, who has scaled Mount Everest twice and is a local mountaineering legend in northern Iran. He invited us to his home for tea and proudly showed us three fossilized crustaceans, which looked like some type of clam. He pointed toward the lofty peaks in the distance and said, through Mohsen's translation, "I found these on the peak of a nearby mountain, over 14,000 feet high."

To account for these fossils at such high elevation, either the ocean floor had to have been raised by more than 14,000 feet, or the ocean at one time was more than two-and-a-half miles above current sea level. Had we stumbled upon compelling evidence of Noah's Flood?

I asked Rasul if he knew of anywhere in these mountains where the rotten egg smell of sulfur could be found, as Ed Davis had described.

"Yes," he said, through Mohsen's translation. "On the other side of the mountain, as you climb up toward Takht-e-Soleiman, there are hot springs with just such an odor."

I sipped my tea while shooting furtive glances at the rest of the team. They were sitting on a scrap of Persian carpet smiling wryly. I continued the questions.

"Rasul, Ed Davis spoke of a place where they tie prayer flags on a tree."

"Yes, here in Rudbarak there used to be a tree where people tied prayer cloths, but the tree is gone now due to homes being built there."

My heart was now pumping blood like the rushing river outside the window. "Do you know of anyone finding wood on the mountain?"

He nodded and said, "On the peak of Soleiman there is wood. I have seen it many times . . . it is old wood."

I then asked if he knew of the ark of Noah being on the mountain.

He looked at Mohsen with a puzzled look on his face and said no, he knew nothing of the ark, but it seemed to provoke an awkward moment for everyone, and I knew that the questions were over for the time being.

We stayed at a spartan climber's hostel that night, and Mohsen told us to say nothing of being Americans.

The next morning, Rasul led us expertly into the dizzying heights of the nearby mountains. We had mules to carry our heavy gear, but it was nevertheless a steep, taxing, uphill climb of seven hours to the base camp. At about 11,000 feet, we pitched camp in a saddled canyon surrounded by majestic mountain peaks. After that climb, we had no trouble getting to sleep.

THE VIEW FROM DOOMSDAY POINT

The next morning, it was still dark as we headed out to climb the 15,300-foot peak called Takht-e-Soleiman. At a little over 13,000 feet, I began to notice that I was laboring to catch my breath. This was alarming because on earlier expeditions I had always been able to keep pace and usually led the pack. I told Steve, Mike, and Rasul to continue climbing to the summit to try to find the wood that reportedly had been seen up there, and that Doug and I would scout out the place that Ed Davis had called Doomsday Point.

Two hours later, Doug and I stood close to where Ed Davis had stood in 1943 when he claimed that he had seen the ark. Dr. Ed Holroyd had previously identified this spot, which is perched on a spiny, steep-flanked mountain known as Mian-Se-Chal. Doug pulled out a photocopy of a hand-drawn map that Ed Davis had crafted in 1986 with the help of artist Elfred Lee. Davis was an engineer, and the map was a remarkably detailed recollection of what he had seen. Doug held the drawing in front of us as we both identified correlating matches on the surrounding terrain.

"There's the dry lake bed Ed described," Doug called out, pointing to a spot maybe half a mile below where we stood. I called at-

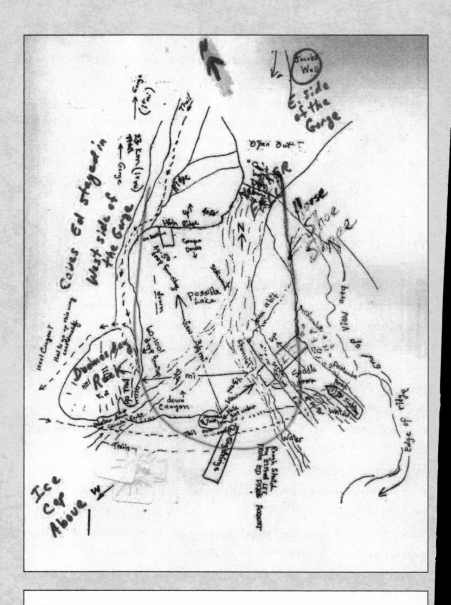

This is part of a sketch done by Ed Davis with the help of Elfred Lee in July 1986. This is Ed's recollection of the area where he saw the ark. COPYRIGHT © ELFRED LEE.

tention to several ridges, peaks, and streams that all seemed to match the details of the map. The sharp drop-off was there, with its spilling streams descending into a deep gorge that framed an ever-present bank of clouds. These clouds were a distinct, local, atmospheric condition that Ed had mentioned and that we now associated with the mountain's proximity to the Caspian Sea.

Feature by feature, Ed Davis's map seemed to correlate with what we could observe in the landscape—distances between ridges, ice cap directions, ridgeline contours, and other landmarks. As each geographic characteristic matched up, our degree of confidence increased that we had found the Ed Davis site—and that his description of what he had seen was accurate. My labored breathing from the day's climb was now eclipsed by a surge of adrenaline.

Looking closely at the map, we calculated where we ought to find the lower object that Ed had seen, but there was nothing there, only tons of loose rock draping over craggy ledges and runoffs. Next, we scanned the upper ridgeline where Ed Davis said he had spotted the ark as he squinted into a sleeting snowstorm so long ago . . . *and it was there!*

Jutting from a hillside, three-quarters of a mile or so across the ravine, we saw what looked like a dark, giant, stone bird poised for flight. We saw the beam-like structures that Ed had mentioned, but they were not as I expected from his testimony; they were more tangled and less impressive. There was no door or obvious decks, such as Ed had described, nor did the structure have the boxy shape that one would expect from the ark. But it was nonetheless remarkable, and Doug and I stood in bewilderment and awe as our minds tried to wrap around the possibility of it all.

For a long, silent moment, we stared gap-jawed across the ravine at the massive stone sentinel. Was it anything other than a natural jumble of dark rocks that only appeared to be a collection of petrified beams? Was it merely another natural geological formation, as every other "ark sighting" had turned out to be, or could it possibly be—was there any chance that it was—the corpse of Noah's ark?

As he gazed across the valley, Doug said, "Well, I could see that if the ground were covered in snow, you could sure mistake that big dark rock for an ark."

It was getting late, so we hiked down a rocky ravine to return to camp and wait for the others to join us. We would have to wait until the following morning to climb the steep rise that cradled what we were now confident was the Ed Davis object.

As we made our way down to camp, Doug and I split up to cover more terrain. He skirted the ridgeline to the right, looking for signs of the second object that Ed Davis had seen. I went down the lower route, scouting for anything else that might prove interesting.

As I hiked down, I started to get really thirsty, so I stopped to get a drink of water from a cascading glacier melt that tumbled down the mountainside and had eroded a big cave-like hole into the edge of the glacier thirty feet below where I stood. I could hear the water crashing into a subterranean lake inside the dark opening. As I stepped over some small rocks at the stream's edge, I lost my footing and found myself hurtling down a sheet of black ice, headed straight toward the ten-foot-wide mouth of the cave. (It was what we refer to in mountain climbing parlance as an unsurvivable event.) At the last split second before I reached the point of no return, I saw a jutting rock the size of a basketball frozen in the ice.

Amazingly, my boot slammed into it, stopping my descent. As icy water washed under me, I flung my other leg over to some stable rocks and crawled up and out.

Doug soon showed up, and I told him about my narrowly averted disaster. He didn't say much, but he snapped a few pictures of the glacier and the black hole.

By the time we made it back to camp, it was late afternoon, but Mike, Steve, and Rasul had not yet returned from the summit. We had heard several rock avalanches high on the mountain all day long and were concerned for the group's safety. However, they showed up safe and sound before dark and showed us some scraps of wood they had gathered, about the size of what you'd get out of a wood chipper, and also a small piece of what looked like a fragment of ancient pottery. The wood was soft and weathered, and though it looked old it did not appear to be ancient, but we packed it away to have it tested.[†]

Doug and I told the others about our discoveries, and we discussed our plans for the next day. When I pointed up the mountain in the general direction of the large, black object, Rasul turned away without saying a word. I remember thinking that this was very odd behavior from someone who had been so attentive and gracious with us.

....

[†] After our return to the United States, I had these wood samples tested by Beta Analytic, of Miami, Florida, the world's largest provider of radiocarbon dating to the scientific community. Beta determined the age of the wood to be between 355 and 565 years old (AD 1440–1650). Obviously, wood that is only several hundred years old (rather than several thousand years or more) would not be fragments directly from Noah's ark, but the discovery of this wood almost three miles above sea level (and well above the treeline) raised an interesting scenario in my mind. If the Ed Davis object was considered the actual site of the remains of Noah's ark, according to local tradition, it seems logical that four or five hundred years ago the indigenous mountain dwellers might have erected some type of shrine or altar near the site of the ark. How else would we account for the presence of such old wood, and an old piece of pottery, on a steep, icy mountainside at such a high elevation?

Another strange thing had happened earlier in the day when we encountered an Iranian climber who spoke very good English. Without our telling him anything about why we were on the mountain, he told us that others had come looking for beams high on the mountain, but that he had personally burned every bit of wood that high up on Soleiman. Obviously, that did not include the wood that Steve, Mike, and Rasul had brought back from the summit.

THE FINAL ASCENT

Sleep was troublesome that night as a persistent cold wind, mixed with a spatter of rain, ripped at our tents. But we were greeted the next morning by a glorious sunrise, and soon we were off to see the Ed Davis object up close.

I was worried that Rasul might not think kindly of our poking around on the mountain, so after discussing it with my partners, we decided to leave our guide asleep at the base camp and head up to the Ed Davis site on our own for some early morning reconnaissance.

From our camp at 11,000 feet, it was a steep climb over loose rock, but within the hour we had ascended to the 12,500-foot elevation where the massive formation stood. In some places, the sides of the object looked like the petrified remains of an old Spanish galleon. The dark rocks had a burnished look with what appeared like bark and other wood-like characteristics. It was remarkable. No one in our group showed much emotion at what we had found. There was a moment of almost reverent silence. Then the excitement began to build.

"I have no clue how this was formed," Doug said as he ran his hand over the surface of the rock. "But what if there *were* an ark here at one time, and over time silt and sediment from the mountain settled within the ark. The wood would eventually go away and what would remain would be the rock."

"Boy, it's convincing," I said. "You can almost see knotholes up there."

We examined the surface of the sheer face and marveled at the striations and colors that looked every bit like the mottled imperfections of wood. The upward lines and uniform widths gave the appearance of closely spaced beams with sediment-filled gaps in between.

Doug dislodged a hunk of rock, maybe sixteen inches long, from the top of the formation. He handed it down to Steve and said, "That looks like a piece of wood, guys."

When I saw it, it almost took my breath away. It looked like a split log you would toss in the fireplace.

"In every particular," Steve said, "it looks like it could have come right off a tree."

"It's got a circular grain to it," Doug added as we all gathered around for a closer look.

"Look at the grain on the end," I said. "It looks like split wood, like tree rings."

"I can tell you that it's a lot heavier than wood," Steve said as he maneuvered the object for our inspection.

"It's not wood now," Doug added.

Steve shook his head. "No, it's not wood now."

After I had filmed most of the action, I stopped and looked back across the ravine toward Doomsday Point. I tried to imagine a young army sergeant peering through the falling snow, his eyes straining to see the object where we now stood. Because of the bad weather, he'd never gotten this close, but the contrast between the blackened object and the backdrop of snow must have made an impressive sight. I could see how he believed until the day he died that it was Noah's ark.

For the next half hour, we explored the site, scaling the formation and taking photographs from many different angles and of many interesting features. We were scheduled to leave the mountain later that morning and had no way of knowing whether we would ever be able to return, so we hurriedly did everything we could think of to record what we had seen. The time quickly got away from us, and by 10:00 AM we were already late for our agreed-upon departure.

As we explored the site, I allowed my mind to begin to ponder the possibilities of what we had found. *If this was indeed the ark,* I thought, *then what might we deduce from the biblical account of the Flood and the evidence at hand?*

Somewhere in ancient times, thousands of years ago, a drenching rain came in silver sheets as water erupted from the bowels of the earth and sprayed high in the air. Pelting rain split by claps of thunder were the last sounds heard by all things that crept, flew, walked, or slithered on the earth. The air that had once filled their lungs was now replaced by an onslaught of unrelenting, overpowering water. An unsurvivable event of the greatest magnitude. Everything drowned except that which was aboard the ark. Under a frothing, unabated sea, the primordial soil soon became soft, thick, silted mire.

One hundred and fifty days after the first raindrops heralded the wrath of God's judgment, the seas receded and the enormous bulk of the ark's wide hull settled back to earth. Creaking timbers were greeted by oozing mud as the massive ship settled deep into its final berth.

As the earth dried, the inhabitants of the ark eventually emerged and commenced a great migration across the earth. The ark was abandoned like the shed skin of a lizard.

Nothing in the Bible indicates that any of Noah's descendants considered the ark a relic worthy of worship. It was simply deserted, left to the mercy of time and nature more than two miles above sea level, in a desolate mountain range that the Bible refers to as the mountains of Ararat.

The tar-covered beams of the ark's lower sections were likely entombed in mud caused by the Flood, and were subsequently covered by accumulating dirt, possibly beginning the process of petrifaction.

Four elements are necessary for petrifaction to occur: water, mud, wood, and time—all of which were available in abundance in the case of Noah's ark. The entire ark need not have been entombed in mud for the petrifaction process to be accomplished, only sections. And the appearance of sections are what we seemed to have found.

The massive, tumbledown formation on Mount Soleiman is consistent with what one might reasonably expect to find of the ark after all these years. The ark would be distorted, crumbled in, with the hollow spaces filled with differing sediments, muds, and soil. It's provocative to think that this could be the skeletal carcass of a noble craft that had done its duty and now rested quietly in the upper reaches of a big mountain . . . waiting.

July 27, 2005

Dr. Robert Cornuke
BASE Institute
18580 Augusta Drive
Monument, CO 80132

Dear Dr. Cornuke:

Upon examination of the many photos of the recent expedition to Iran, I am amazed to find what appears to be the remarkable preservation of the formerly wooden structures that comprise the object in question. Although the precise process of petrifaction is for now unknown, such a finding will likely cause much disagreement among geologists as they seek to explain the object that has been found. What should be noted at this point, however, is that wood exposed to atmospheric elements (as well as any other agents promoting degradation of wood) for thousands of years would mandate that the wood be altered from its original organic state in order to preserve at least its structural form(s). If the original wood was cut/shaped to form components for a man-made object, logically it would follow that a petrifaction process, whereby inorganic components (e.g., calcium carbonate, silica) are substituted for organic components, could then allow that such a man-made object be preserved as well.

Since petrifaction is a process associated with infiltration by water containing dissolved inorganic matter for replacement, and since the setting of the find does not suggest a typical presence of water for immersion, it is likely that the controversy of the nature of this object will not be easily resolved by geologists any time soon.

Sincerely,

Paul M. Feinberg

Paul M. Feinberg, Ph.D.
Adjunct Lecturer in Geology
Hunter College
New York, N.Y.

Letter from geologist Dr. Paul Feinberg after his review of photographs
from the Mount Soleiman expedition.

❦

After posing for several touristy photographs to commemorate our discovery, we scavenged a few souvenir-size bits of rock, and what appeared to us to be petrified wood, and prepared to return to base camp. We all felt that we were too spent to lug any of the big, heavy pieces down the mountain, and we also had the practical concern of how we would transport such a large specimen out of the country. Based on past experience, I was really paranoid about getting arrested, as I had been on a previous trip to Iran. My main concern was to get our cameras out of Iran without drawing any attention that might get our pictures confiscated by the authorities.

Thankfully, our departure through Tehran came off without a hitch, and we were greeted with great enthusiasm when we returned to the United States. Everyone to whom we showed our pictures and samples in the first couple of weeks responded with interest and excitement.

EVALUATING THE EVIDENCE

I soon discovered that there were differing opinions as to what would constitute conclusive analysis of the samples. I showed pictures of the beams and other parts of the structure to several geologists, one of whom told me it had all the appearances of petrified wood. Another said it did not, that it was metamorphosed sedimentary rock. Some suggested it might be a cast, displaying the original shape of the wood.

I learned that when wood is swallowed in a landslide, covered by a mudflow, or buried by flood deposits, the wood fiber decays and may be replaced by inorganic mineral deposits. In this process, the composition changes from organic (wood) to inorganic (rock or mineral).

Sometimes, the mineralization occurs only in the empty spaces between the wood fibers. This is called *permineralization*. When the wood itself dissolves and is completely replaced by minerals from the soil, the resulting structure is known as *replacement*.

Sometimes, the caked mud encasing the wood leaves a gap in the harder matrix around the wood, which in time fills in with another mineral, making a natural cast, or *pseudomorph*, of the original form. All of these processes either turn the wood to stone or make a mold-casting, resulting in a mineral form of the original wood shape. When it's all said and done, C-14 radiocarbon testing methods are of no use in establishing the age of the rock because there is no longer any carbon to test.[1]

The common denominator for all of the geologists we spoke with was that their opinions were influenced by their presuppositions about the age of the earth, their understanding of petrifaction (primarily how much time it would take to petrify wood), and their belief in or rejection of the story of Noah's ark. In one conversation that Doug Scherling had with a geologist in Colorado, he was told that the samples couldn't be petrified wood because they weren't round like a tree would be. When Doug pointed out that these beams would have been handcrafted in the construction of the ark, the geologist said that that was impossible because the petrifaction process would have begun before mankind inhabited the earth.

It should be noted here that if the formation we found on the mountainside in Iran is indeed Noah's ark, then a whole set of factors would be present that do not apply to any other subfossil. First, the wood is located in thin, cold air at an elevation of 12,500 feet, above the timberline, where no trees grow. Second, the original wood would be antediluvian (pre-Flood) gopherwood, and we have no idea what that species of wood even looks like. Third, Noah covered the ark inside and out with pitch (possibly an oil-based substance). What effect this coating would have on the preservation of the wood, I cannot say, but interestingly, in 1930, a complete carcass of a wooly rhinoceros was recovered from an oil seep in Sarunia, Poland, and it was in a remarkable state of preservation.[2]

Because of these unusual factors pertaining to the ark—there's nothing like it to compare it to—it seems very difficult to either confirm or reject the data in relation to what we found. It may ultimately fall into the realm of faith, along with other historical information from the Bible that we can't absolutely prove. And maybe that's the way God intended it.

ARK FEVER LIVES ON

After my return from Iran, I had only a few precious days to finish this final chapter before the production deadline—and those days were a whirlwind of activity. I didn't have enough time to conduct all the tests, confer with all the scientific experts, and ponder all the implications of what we found. But I'm content to let the book go to press because I know that the story will go on.

I'm not about to make a dogmatic pronouncement about what we found on Mount Soleiman, but I can say that I have a high level of confidence that it was the same thing that Ed Davis saw.

After seeing the video we recorded on the mountain, a close friend asked, "How are you going to convince the world that this is the ark?"

I replied, "I don't intend to try to convince anyone of anything."

I'm happy to share what I've found and let other people draw their own conclusions. I'm not sure that we'll ever be able to prove beyond a shadow of a doubt that we've found the lost ark of Noah, but I hope that this new evidence will inspire people to take another look at the historical reality of the Flood and its place in human history. Down through the ages, and especially in our day and age, the story of Noah and the ark has been looked at by an unbelieving world as a rusted-out myth, ignored by some, ridiculed by others, and believed by but a few.

Jesus Christ predicted that the story of Noah would one day be ridiculed as myth and legend—just as the story of Jesus' own life and his impending return to earth would be mocked and disregarded:

> As it was in the days of Noah, so it will be at the coming of the Son of Man. For in the days before the flood, people were eating and drinking, marrying and giving in marriage, up to the day Noah entered the ark; and they knew nothing about what would happen until the flood came and took them all away. That is how it will be at the coming of the Son of Man. (Matthew 24:37-39, NIV)

Some people will rejoice at what we found on Mount Soleiman; others will mock; and most may not care one way or another. But for the four of us who stood on that mountainside, who touched the rock and considered the possibilities, our dreams will forever be filled with wonder—just as Ed Davis's dreams were filled—until the day we meet our Maker, and we find out for absolute certain if it really was Noah's ark.

WHAT IF ... ?

I've dedicated the past five years to posing questions and seeking answers in the areas of science, philosophy, history, archaeology, and religion. My passion is exploration, observation, and dialogue in these fascinating worlds. As part of my journey, I've studied dozens of Flood stories from ancient cultures and I've examined volumes of scientific evidence for a worldwide cataclysmic deluge. Noah's Flood is a fantastic study, whether you view it as historic truth or ancient legend.

When I got an afternoon call from Bob Cornuke and his team, I was given a one-evening opportunity to view a profound collection of images and artifacts—a once-in-a-lifetime chance to tangibly observe, question, and consider what if . . . ?

What I saw, heard, and touched was truly profound. It's not that I beheld conclusive proof for the ark of Noah, but I witnessed compelling evidence that shook my soul. What if a story like this could jump-start journeys for millions who've grown numb in our passive culture? What if we returned to authentic dialogue about the profound questions of life?

I viewed a monolith of apparently petrified beams resting thousands of feet above the tree line on a mountain in Iran. What is it? Any way you slice it, this is exciting stuff. It may only be the remnants of an ancient structure resting in the middle of nowhere at 12,500 feet, but what if . . . ?

I held three fossilized clams found at 14,000 feet in the same mountain range in Iran. Why are they there? Whatever your worldview about geologic history, this again is exciting stuff. I've read articles and studied photos of marine fossils found atop other major mountain ranges of the world, but now I held actual specimens that had come out of the field only days earlier. What if . . . ?

Remarkably, somewhere in the past one hundred years or so, "enlightened" scholars started referring to the hundreds of Flood stories as mere myths of simple, ancient peoples. The notion of a true global flood was placed just below Bigfoot on the shelves of academic credibility. Somehow, the establishment of science, philosophy, and humanist thought determined that an ancient cataclysmic deluge is a faith-based legend for weak-minded fundamentalist-types. Why? Who wrote the new rules for enlightened critical thinking?

My sincere hope is that Bob Cornuke's recent discoveries on a mountain in Iran will spark many of us to return to the adventure of existence, wherever the evidence leads us. . . .

Randall Niles
Director of Operations
All About GOD Ministries, Inc.

A FINAL WORD

Nothing in the Bible indicates that the ark of Noah survived after its divinely appointed use. But even if it did, and even if what we found on Mount Soleiman turns out to be the remains of the ark, we mustn't allow this discovery to distract us from faith in God. More than likely, some people would flock to see any wood fragments said to be from the ark, and these artifacts might become objects of veneration. There are those who would believe that its splintered remains could cure their ailments or bring good fortune. The wood could become an idol with a cult following.

This very thing happened in the Old Testament with another relic called the bronze serpent, which Moses made when the children of Israel were wandering in the wilderness along the border of Edom (Numbers 21:4-9). The people complained to Moses that he had brought them to the blistering desert to die. They craved water and moaned bitterly about the bread God had provided for them. The complaints angered God, who sent "fiery serpents" among the people. When the snakes bit them, many of the Israelites died.

The Israelites made a quick attitude adjustment, admitting that they had sinned and pleading with Moses to ask God for help. God told Moses to make a bronze serpent and place it on a wooden pole so that those who were bitten by snakes could gaze at it and be spared. Many years later, the ancient icon became an object of veneration. When people burned incense before the bronze figure, King Hezekiah ordered it to be ground to dust and destroyed (2 Kings 18:4).

Two thousand years ago, a sinless man was staked on a wooden cross as a final solution to death. He alone deserves our worship, not a bronze snake stuck on a pole or an old boat decaying on some remote mountaintop. Noah's ark should only be looked upon as a physical reminder of God's amazing faithfulness and power. The ark itself possesses no mystical power, but it represents a special act of God, a hinge in history that exemplifies the heart of God's amazing grace.

THE ARK THAT MATTERS

There is another ark to be found if you are willing to look for it. It is not a wooden ship lost on the slopes of a remote mountain in the ancient land of Ararat. It is the real ark, the only one that can truly save you. There is no need to trek over icy mountain peaks in Turkey or Iran to find it. The real ark is right in front of you with its doors open wide.

My dad found this real ark one day in Prescott, Arizona. I remember walking into a doctor's office where my mom clutched Dad's hand. They both sat in silent, tense anticipation as a doctor scratched some notes on a medical chart. Dad was shockingly thin; his robust face, normally tan and chiseled, was pale and hollow. I had always known him as an imposing figure and often shook at the sound of his commanding voice when I was young. Now that voice was hesitant as he asked, "What's wrong with me, Doctor?"

Cancer is one of those words that rolls easily off the tongue but chills the soul when spoken by a doctor. No one is ever prepared to hear it when it applies to them. The doctor gave Dad between two and six months to live. When my father heard the prognosis, he exhaled slowly. Mom gasped, then reached in her purse for a handkerchief. The doctor tucked the metal clipboard under his arm and looked at Dad without a trace of emotion.

"Mr. Cornuke," he said, "you will soon meet your Maker. If I were you, I'd make the appropriate preparations."

What a cold, insensitive bedside manner, I thought. But then I realized that the doctor had given my father wise counsel. God warns people again and again that they should prepare for death, but most never listen. Most people take more time planning a two-week vacation than they do their journey into eternity. So it was with Dad. He never saw death lurking behind him; instead, he always looked forward and took his borrowed time here on earth for granted.

Now that death was breathing down his neck, I felt that it was time for us to talk. My dad and I had never been close. I remember no long walks together or times of sitting on his knee. He was more on the gruff-and-tough side. He thought that his three sons should be forged to face an unkind world, not coddled. But he was my dad, and though we never shared the closeness I craved, we were bound together by whatever innate link exists between father and son.

One of my biggest regrets is that I never made more than a token attempt to discuss God with my father. The only job my father ever had was as a bartender. For forty-five years, he spent his nights in a smoky bar, serving drinks to clientele who were typically less than interested in anything having to do with church. That was just fine with Dad. Whenever I ever tried to raise the subject of faith, my father would lift his hand in protest. Our personal beliefs remained private.

Mom stood and left the room, pulling more wads of tissue from her purse as she went. Drawing a chair up to Dad, I looked into eyes that were raw with worry.

"Dad, can we talk?" I had never approached him like this, and the moment was awkward for both of us.

He looked away, saying nothing. Even in his failing physical state he brought trepidation to my heart. I felt like a young boy again, and just being with him made me anxious. Feeling as if an elephant were sitting on my chest, I forced out the question, "Do you believe in God?"

He kept a fixed stare away from me, as if resolute about his fate.

"What good is it now?" His words were a rope sliding through loose fingers, letting a boat slip away from the dock and slowly drift out to sea.

I rubbed my sweaty hands together. I had spoken countless times in churches, on television, and on the radio about the Bible, but with my dad I was stumbling all over the place. *What is wrong with me?* I wondered. *Why is this so hard?*

I pulled myself together as best I could, telling my dad that, like him, Noah had three sons, and together they had built an ark. One day, with his family and his animal cargo safe on board, a small drop of rain had spiraled out of a dark cloudy sky, and a deluge of rain soon followed. Lightning crashed and the water rose higher and higher. The flooding began. Men ran from the fields where they labored, and women desperately clutched their babies. All waded through floating debris to the side of the ark, but the big door was closed. People frantically beat on the side of the ark until their fists were bloodied, but their muffled cries went unanswered. The water just kept rising.

Their fate was sealed when the door of that ark was closed by God's mighty hand. At that moment, a life-and-death sentence was passed. Everyone inside would be saved, and everyone outside would die.

I told my father that we have an ark today named Jesus Christ.

For Dad, it was just as it was in Noah's time. The doctor's words had stirred the dark storm clouds forming on the horizon, and a flood was sure to come. I asked Dad if he wanted to be on the ark of Christ before the door of his life closed forever.

He lowered his head and moaned, "I am not a good man. God doesn't know me and I don't know him."

I told my dad the story of Christ walking from the town of Jericho and seeing blind beggars along the road. Those beggars no doubt sat in filthy clothes that crawled with flies. The crowds that passed the beggars probably held their sleeves over their faces to mask the obnoxious smell. But the beggars cried out, "Jesus, Jesus," and our Lord touched them and healed them (Matthew 20:29-34).

"Dad," I said, "you and I and everyone in this world are filthy from sin. But if we call out to Jesus, he will hear us, forgive our sins, and give us eternal life in heaven."

Dad reached up and took my hand in his. His once vice-like grip had weakened. He gathered words from his laboring soul and said, "Jesus, Jesus." Tears streamed down his face as he said, louder, "I want forgiveness for what I've done."

I led him in prayer as he confessed his wrongs and embraced salvation. Tears continued to flow, washing away deep furrows of worry and years of regret. We laughed and cried for sheer joy that his eternal destiny was secure on the Ark. I had never witnessed such a moment in all my life. I could not fathom that my own father would open the floodgates of his heart and pour out his soul at God's feet.

My dad found the real Ark and walked on board. He was safe now for his impending eternal voyage, which began thirty-six hours later when his heart stopped beating and he drew his final breath on earth.

The world has been looking for Noah's ark for a very long time. My dad found the real Ark before its door closed forever. It was not lost in an inaccessible place high on a mountain or in a distant and forbidden land. The real Ark was found where it had been waiting all along.

It was only a prayer away.

NOTES

Foreword
1. Quoted by Rex Geissler in the preface to *The Explorers of Ararat*, B.J. Corbin, comp. (Long Beach, Calif.: Great Commission Illustrated Books, 1999).

Chapter 2: The Eyewitness
1. The account of Ed Davis's testimony was compiled from a number of sources, including several videotaped interviews conducted by Don Shockey; two transcripts, one by Shockey, the other by Robin Simmons; a cassette recording from the Jim Irwin archives; and supporting documentation from the Rice University Fondren Library. Special thanks go to Brian Park, a research coordinator with BASE Institute, who reviewed all of the accounts for accuracy and consistency.

Chapter 5: The Phone Call
1. J. D. Douglas, et. al., eds., *New Bible Dictionary* (Leicester: InterVarsity; Wheaton, Ill.: Tyndale, 1982), 1106.

2. Dr. Lee Spencer and Dr. Jean Luc Lienard, "The Search for Noah's Ark." http://origins.swau.edu/papers/global/noah/default.html.

3. Bill Crouse, "Noah's Ark Sources and Alleged Sightings," in B. J. Corbin (compiler), *The Explorers of Ararat* (Long Beach, Calif.: Great Commission Illustrated Books, 1999), 49.

4. David M. Rohl, *Legend: The Genesis of Civilization, A Test of Time,* vol. 2. (London: Arrow, 1998).

Chapter 6: Remapping the Search

1. Bill Crouse, "Noah's Ark Sources," 49.

2. James Bryce, *Transcaucasia and Ararat* (London: Macmillan, 1877), 232.

3. Bill Crouse, "Noah's Ark Sources," 47.

Chapter 7: East of Shinar

1. *Herodotus: the Histories,* Aubrey de Selincourt, trans. (Baltimore: Penguin, 1954).

2. Roman Ghirshman, *Persia: The Immortal Kingdom* (Greenwich, Conn.: New York Graphic Society, 1971), 20.

3. W. B. Fisher, ed., *The Cambridge History of Iran,* vol. 1 (London: Cambridge University Press, 1968), 294, 309–323, 372.

Chapter 9: The Photos

1. *Zondervan Pictorial Encyclopedia of the Bible* (Grand Rapids: Zondervan, 1975).

2. *Cambridge History of Iran,* vol. 2 (Cambridge: Cambridge University Press, 1985), 72.

3. *Jewish Encyclopedia,* Isidore Singer, ed. (New York and London: Funk & Wagnall's, 1902).

Chapter 10: Meeting the Mountain

1. John Warwick Montgomery, *The Quest for Noah's Ark* (Minneapolis: Bethany Fellowship, 1972), 62.

Chapter 16: The Map, the SEAL, and the "Object"

1. David M. Rohl, *Legend,* 104.

Chapter 20: One Last Try

1. Lloyd R. Bailey, *Noah: The Person and the Story in History and Tradition* (Columbia: University of South Carolina Press, 1989), 65.

Chapter 21: Is It the Ark—at Last?

1. Adapted from *Rocks, Minerals, Gems, Crystals, Fossils: The Complete Collector's Companion,* Harriet Stewart Jones, ed. (Edison, N J.: Chartwell, 1995), 115.
2. Carl O. Dunbar and Karl M. Waage, *Historical Geology* (New York: J. Wiley, 1969), 37.

. Bob Cornuke and his horse take a break on the slopes of Mount Ararat. COPYRIGHT © ROBERT CORNUKE.

. The McGivern object can be seen in the lower part of the photograph. There is no ark—only dirt and rock. COPYRIGHT © DIGITAL GLOBE INC and

SHAMROCK TRINITY CORP.

3. During World War II, Sergeant Ed Davis was working on supply-line roads in Iran when his young Iranian driver told him that the remains of Noah's ark were embedded in snow high on a mountain in the distance. PHOTO COURTESY OF DR. DONALD SHOCKEY.

4. Ed Davis (in the middle) with two unidentified friends on a sightseeing tour of Iran during World War II. PHOTO COURTESY OF DR. DONALD SHOCKEY.

5. Ed Davis with Bob Cornuke in 1988, just before Ed's polygraph test in Albuquerque. COPYRIGHT © ROBERT CORNUKE.

6. A high mountain lake near the summit of Mount Sabalon in Iran. COPYRIGHT © ROBERT CORNUKE.

7. Bob Cornuke on the ascent of Mount Soleiman, July 2005. COPYRIGHT © ROBERT CORNUKE.

8. The dark mass in the center of this photo is believed to be part of the object that Ed Davis saw in 1943. COPYRIGHT © ROBERT CORNUKE.

9. Downhill close-up view of the Ed Davis object. Note the unusual formation along the top edge. COPYRIGHT © ROBERT CORNUKE.

10. Uphill view showing possible hull-like shape. For size comparison, notice Steve Crampton on the lower left side of the object.
COPYRIGHT © ROBERT CORNUKE.

11. Expedition team members Steve Crampton, Bob Cornuke, and Mike Morrison. Note the color contrast between the object and the surrounding terrain. Photo by team member Doug Scherling. COPYRIGHT © ROBERT CORNUKE.

12. & 13. Note the grain and other wood-like characteristics of what are believed to be petrified wood beams. COPYRIGHT © ROBERT CORNUKE.

14. Upward thrust of what appears to be closely spaced petrified beams. Could these be from Noah's ark? COPYRIGHT © ROBERT CORNUKE.

15. Fragment of beam believed to be petrified wood. Note what appears to be a hand-cut notch at the bottom. COPYRIGHT © ROBERT CORNUKE.

16. Seashell fossils found at 14,000-foot elevation by Rasul, our Iranian mountain guide. How were shells deposited 2½ miles above sea level? COPYRIGHT © ROBERT CORNUKE.

17. What appears to be a shard of ancient pottery, found at 15,300-foot elevation on Mount Soleiman by Mike Morrison and Steve Crampton. COPYRIGHT © ROBERT CORNUKE.